RISING TIDES

Caitlin Press Inc.
8100 Alderwood Road,
Halfmoon Bay, BC VON 1Y1
www.caitlin-press.com

Illustrations by Deblekha Guin
Text design by Shed Simas / Onça Design
Cover design by Vici Johnstone
Printed in Canada

Caitlin Press Inc. acknowledges financial su
and the Canada Council for the Arts, and
the British Columbia Arts Council and

Canada Council Conseil des arts
for the Arts du Canada

Library and Archives Canada Catal

Title: Rising tides : reflections for
    Sandilands.
Other titles: Rising tides (Halfm
Names: Sandilands, Catriona, ed
Identifiers: Canadiana 20190144
Subjects: LCSH: Climatic chang
Classification: LCC PS8237.C65

# Rising Tides

## REFLECTIONS FOR
## CLIMATE CHANGING TIMES

Edited by Catriona Sandilands

CAITLIN PRESS

# Contents

## What We Have Lost

## What Worries Us

## What We May Understand

## What We Imagine

# Territorial Acknowledgement

## LEVI WILSON & EMILY MENZIES

My name is Levi Wilson. Through my grandmother I am a member of the Gitga'at First Nation, with strong familial connections to the Hwlitsum and Lamalcha peoples. I would like to acknowledge the shared, asserted, and unceded territory of the Penelakut, Lamalcha, other Hul'q'umi'num'-speaking peoples, and any other peoples who hold rights and responsibilities in and around the territory that is now known as Galiano Island, as well as the treatied territory of the Tsawwassen First Nation. I would like to acknowledge the privilege of living, learning, and caring for one another and the land in their traditional territory.

Acknowledgements today are an adaptation of a traditional protocol that is observed by many Indigenous groups across what is now known as Canada. At their best, acknowledgements achieve the goal of recognizing the peoples who have lived and hold rights and responsibilities in the region that the sharer is now in. For example, when I am in the region that surrounds the Salish Sea, I include in my acknowledgements words such as "shared" and "asserted" to represent how the peoples here live through the seasonal round, and that the Indigenous inhabitants have never stopped knowing, believing in, and, most importantly, acting on their rights and responsibilities.

*Why is a territorial acknowledgement critical in a book seeking to inspire and equip people hoping to survive and even thrive during a time of climate chaos? Done right, a territorial acknowledgement is more than just a way to identify oneself as an ally in the struggle for self-determination among Indigenous Peoples. By insisting on acknowledging place, and the peoples of our place, territorial acknowledgements also provide an opportunity for us to learn about histories, current politics, teachings, and relationships that can contribute to rebuilding ecological, social, and economic sustainability in our communities.*

Acknowledgements are living documents, meant to grow and change, much as we as people grow and change over time. Done by rote, an acknowledgement quickly becomes meaningless: it stops growing. What I really want you to take away is how I have built this practice and changed the wording of my acknowledgement based on conversations with and challenges by those who have heard it. For example, in many of my early versions, I included a "thank you" to those First Nations mentioned "for living on their land," but after I had listened to and tried out acknowledgements for a month in every single high school class that I teach, one of my students nervously called in this wording. She felt that, by including a thank you, I was assuming that the Nations listed welcome and enjoy all of the disparate peoples that now inhabit their territory. I invited my students to help figure out a solution, and, over fifty suggestions later, we decided to take out the "thank you" and replace it with "acknowledge the privilege."

*Sharing a territorial acknowledgement is one way to foster awareness, community, leadership skills, and hope for the future, all of which, I believe, are integral to riding the storms of climate change instead of drowning in them. When we take the time to learn about our place and who the Indigenous Peoples of our places are, we build relationships with survivors of the colonial apocalypse, with the keepers of knowledge about how to live within the means of our local ecosystems: both how it has been and how it is now. By learning how people have lived, for thousands of years, in the places we call home, we gain insight into how to weather future change.*

Acknowledgements are an expression of our relationship to the land, no matter whose territory we find ourselves in. If it is a place that you have lived in for a long time, then the acknowledgement will be longer, more complex, and more thought out than one that is done in a place you may be visiting. The first few times a person engages in this practice it will feel rough; it should be a chance to learn and, in the future, to show that learning. An acknowledgement is a practice rather than just a protocol. Any person giving an acknowledgement needs to work and reflect, to try again and again, and to get better and more comfortable with giving acknowledgements as something that requires practice.

*Beginning with acknowledgements, settlers can take the opportunity to learn social survival skills that have helped people not only endure genocidal policies but also live well, here, for thousands of years, such as using humour to overcome adversity, and the importance of holding extended family networks dear. We may learn how to prioritize relationships over clocks, mutual respect over control, our role as part of a collective over individual greed. We may ponder why so many First Nations are traditionally governed by matrilineal, if not matriarchal, social structures, as well as by clan systems that cross otherwise separate Nations, and how these structures may help foster co-operation even in the face of dire hardship and family breakdowns.*

By opening *Rising Tides* with my own territorial acknowledgement for the place the book was born, I am hoping to begin to take acknowledgements back to articulating relationships instead of getting mired in politics—back to helping people understand where they are and how they come to be there. As much as I enjoyed crafting my version of an acknowledgement for this collection, I was hesitant to put it into something as permanent as a book. Anishinaabe author Hayden King, who helped craft the formal acknowledgement for Ryerson University, has said that he now regrets writing it because "the territorial acknowledgement [can] become very superficial....It sort of fetishizes these actual tangible, concrete treaties. They're not metaphors—they're real institutions, and for us to write and recite a territorial acknowledgement...I think we do a disservice to that treaty and to those nations." I have struggled with how to settle this issue. My response is to try to restart the conversation.

*Hwunitum—the People of Time, or the Hungry Ones—are very good at dominating, controlling and exploiting land, people, and other creatures (see Arnett, 1999). However, we are not great at living sustainably. In fact, Hwunitum culture is predicated on the unwavering belief in progress, in moving on when we have used all we want from a particular place. However, most of us settlers come from ancestors who lived in a different way. They may have shared similarities with the ancestors of Hwulmuhw, the People of the Land, here. In my case, each of my Scottish, Scandinavian, Irish, and English foremothers would have had to have known their place intimately: they knew how to keep their families healthy through knowing and cultivating mutually beneficial relationships with the plant, animal, and human neighbours with whom they shared their place. Now we have come to another great time of change, and we need to recover, rediscover, and share narratives and knowledges of how to be humans who are tied to place.*

Acknowledgements are best understood as snapshots of a specific time. In this framework, change is not just necessary; it is the whole point of engaging in acknowledgement. Please take the acknowledgement I am sharing not as a form to fill out with small changes made to suit your region. Rather, treat what I, with the help of many, have crafted as a set of possibilities and suggestions. Embrace the ability to make mistakes and to learn. Take the time needed to care for this practice. Then extend your practice to "caring for one another and the land."

*We have only one planet, yet we are trashing it by treating our home as if it were merely a way station and we have somewhere else to go. There are so many ways to live, in so many wonderful places, as humans have done since time immemorial. As our places change, so must we. To live sustainably, to be able to survive and thrive over time, we need to live as if we mean to stay. Through sharing stories, we remember how to live in resilience.*

Some people question the validity of territorial acknowledgements, asking, "What is the point when the land will never or can never be returned?" The hopelessness behind this argument reminds me of how some people feel when facing the enormity of climate change.

*Levi's grandpa, Fredrick Levi Wilson, a fisherman renowned up and down the coast, witnessed the decimation of the salmon during his lifetime. When asked how fishing was going, he would say, with a straight face and a smile in his voice: "Haywire, haywire, haywire." Somehow, he managed to convey both the challenge and the unwavering belief that the challenge would be overcome, one way or another. For the sake of our daughter, Gladys Arbutus Wilson, and those to come for the next seven generations, we work to make this dream a reality.*

**The salmon people are survivors, and so are we.**
**Huy tseep q'u.**

## Notes:

Levi's voice is in plain text, Emily's is in italics.

Hayden King, "'I Regret It': Hayden King on Writing Ryerson University's Territorial Acknowledgement," *Unreserved*, CBC Radio, January 20, 2019, https://www.cbc.ca/radio/unreserved/redrawing-the-lines-1.4973363/i-regret-it-hayden-king-on-writing-ryerson-university-s-territorial-acknowledgement-1.4973371.

Chris Arnett, *The Terror of the Coast: Land Alienation and Colonial War on Vancouver Island and the Gulf Islands, 1849–1863* (Vancouver: Talonbooks, 1999).

# Reflections for
# Climate Changing Times

**CATRIONA SANDILANDS**

For many Canadians, any talk of climate change immediately conjures terrifying images of large-scale, apocalyptic transformations: dramatically melting glaciers, persistent catastrophic droughts, small islands submerged by rising sea levels. Recent news reports bring these dire stories very close to home. Heat-related deaths in Quebec. Rapidly shrinking Arctic sea ice and melting permafrost across the North. Unprecedented BC and Alberta wildfires. Areas of severe and ongoing drought in the Prairies. Torrential rainstorms and flooding in Southern Ontario. Rising sea levels and extreme storm surges in Atlantic Canada. According to a recent report by Environment and Climate Change Canada, "both past and future warming in Canada is, on average, about double the magnitude of global warming. Northern Canada has warmed and will continue to warm at more than double the global rate." The apocalyptic images are not just alarmist rhetoric: by pretty clear scientific consensus, there is ample reason to be afraid.

Fear can help inspire courageous, determined acts. We need only look at the current wave of young climate activists who are taking to the streets to protest against government inaction in reducing carbon dioxide emissions or at the Indigenous Elders who are leading the charge against the expansion of fossil fuel developments across the continent. But fear can also be incapacitating, especially when it is so often the only emotion at play in media stories about climate-related disasters. A monolithic diet of fear starves more complex feelings. It does not touch the difficult heart of what so many people are currently experiencing in their everyday lives in these climate changing times: grief, rage, hope, wonder, perplexity, even love. Even more, fixating on fear of a future apocalypse draws attention away from the conditions in which, in Canada, we *already* find ourselves, and also from the underlying causes of climate change: ongoing colonialism, our petroleum-dependent extractive economy, and a lack, in large part, of deep concern for the other creatures with whom we share the continent. These elements of climate change deserve a much fuller airing if we are to move beyond fear into collective reflection, understanding, and action.

The stories that we tell about climate change have an especially important role to play in public conversation. Literary works and other kinds of storytelling can help us to notice, feel, understand, talk about, and respond to the unfolding realities of climate change in ways that better acknowledge the personal complexities of our social and environmental relationships. Recent years have seen a proliferation of novels and stories—especially but not only for young adult readers—that include climate changing worlds. Although for many years, the weight of literary work on global warming has been borne primarily by writers of speculative fiction, increasing scientific consensus and popular awareness of the certainty of both global and local change have helped shift the terrain to include a wider range of forms and genres.

Dystopian, post-apocalyptic writing still has its place in the spectrum of climate fiction, or "cli-fi," but as the evidence mounts, both present and near-future fictions have come to focus increasingly on thornier questions of persistence, adaptation, resistance, and renewal. Climate change stories are no longer, if they ever were, only a matter of speculation; they are also, more and more, not confined to fiction as personal climate testimonies also move into the mainstream. These narrative and poetic forays into issues of loss, survival, and transformation ask about how to create a better society from the conditions in which we currently find ourselves, rather than fantasizing about it all blowing up so we can start again.

Climate-focused fiction, non-fiction, and poetry also open space for us to take a hard look at our daily lives in the context of the large sweep of environmental history. Climate change often becomes real to us in small ways: in changes to our accustomed experiences of seasonal foods and activities; in the plants that can no longer grow where we live and the animals that have left for good (and in the new ones that are now appearing); in mounting anxieties over Lyme disease and West Nile virus; or in the new normalcy of smoke-grey summer skies and submerged homes in floodplain communities in the spring. From there, we may discover that many of these changes are about more than global warming: they are also about the transnational movement of exotic species, the effects of suburban sprawl, or the direct impacts of resource extraction and industrial agriculture on local land and marine ecologies. Also, although these experiences of climate change are not always immediately apocalyptic for everyone, they are often catastrophic for some people more than others. As Kyle Powys Whyte notes, Indigenous Peoples have a lot more intimate experience of apocalypse than many others and understand histories of climate change to include the transformations wrought by genocide and settler agriculture in the nineteenth century as well as those wrought by melting ice in the twenty-first. Sharing climate stories that begin with reflections on our everyday observations, and that genuinely respond to the lived experiences of others, can help us to join these dots better, allowing us to understand climate change as exacerbating ongoing problems of inequality and injustice.

Thoughtful works of art and literature are indispensable tools in this critical, emotionally complex project, and *Rising Tides* is a small response to this large demand. The collection includes forty-three works of short fiction, poetry, and literary non-fiction that together create a constellation of reflections for, and responses to, our climate-changing times. They speak of grief, fear, anger, hope, curiosity, determination, resilience, solidarity. They draw direct and metaphoric connections between personal experiences and planetary crises. Some are raw, some are wistful, some are awestruck. Some are even funny. What the contributors share is a commitment to creating works that draw climate change down into intimate experiences, to show the quotidian textures of its past, present, and future ecological upheavals. They also share an understanding that anthropogenic climate change is neither an isolated nor a new phenomenon. It is linked to settler colonialism, petrocapitalism, industrial pollution and waste, habitat loss, automobility, deforestation, and consumerism. Some of the contributions address the mounting scientific evidence of, for example, ocean acidification and warming, species extirpation and extinction, coastal erosion related to sea level rise, and invasive species proliferation (just to name a few). Others address the social, cultural, and political dimensions of climate change: the relationship between the genocide of the Indigenous Peoples of Turtle Island and ongoing histories of anthropogenic climate alteration; the intimacy of so many of our relations, toxic and otherwise, to fossil fuel production; the heartbreaking but crucial labours of activism; the fraught question of figuring out how to speak with our children about the frightening world in which they are becoming adults; and the ongoing problem of repairing profoundly broken relations to other people and other species.

None of the writings in *Rising Tides* will lead directly to "solving" climate change. This is a large-scale project that requires not only observation and imagination but also political will, thoughtful technology, and economic transformation. We hope, however, that our work will inspire others to reflect more deeply on their own experiences, and to share and talk about them with others. *Rising*

*Tides* prompts us to continue the difficult process of coming to terms with the changes that are already happening, and of transforming the present so that the future may not be as bleak as projected in the most apocalyptic models. We hope that our small stories may have large results.

*Rising Tides is part of the larger project, Storying Climate Change, which can be found at https://storyingclimatechange.com/.*

## Notes:

Environment and Climate Change Canada, *Canada's Changing Climate Report*, 2019, https://changingclimate.ca/CCCR2019/.

Kyle Powys Whyte, "Indigenous Science (Fiction) for the Anthropocene: Ancestral Dystopias and Fantasies of Climate Change Crises," *Environment and Planning E: Nature and Space* 1, no. 1–2 (March 2018): 224–42.

# What We Have Lost

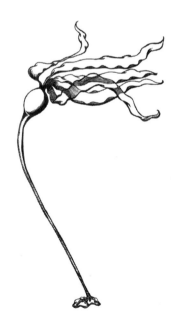

# A Lifetime with Bulb Kelp

**ROSEMARY A. GEORGESON**

I remember as a kid growing up in Georgeson Bay at the bottom end
    of Active Pass
        there used to be so much bulb kelp that it looked
        like you could walk across the bay on it
all of Active Pass was lined on both sides from one end to the other
    with big kelp beds

as the children of a fisherman from a long line of family who call
    the water home
        we were raised to know that these beds of kelp
        were so important to our way of life
the bulb kelp beds were medicines for us
        they helped guide us as we learned to move up and down the
            coast
        they were a place we would look to when we needed food
        like other creatures such as the otter
when he could smell the kelp patches
        he knew his dinner was right there in front of him

kelp supported so much sea life in our pass and on our coast
>    it was home and food for crabs sea urchins abalone and so
>        much more
I always knew that if Dad slowed the boat down by a kelp patch or a
>    reef in the pass
>        we would be having fresh ling cod for dinner.


When I was growing up in Georgeson Bay there was such a strong
>    smell
>        of ocean and life that to me it was just the smell of home
as kids being raised on the shores of Active Pass
>    one of the fastest moving pieces of water on our south coast
we were always being warned by our parents and grandparents and
>    all our old family
>        to stay away from it
>        the water could pull you under so quick
they taught us that if you landed in it you shouldn't fight or panic
>        you should just let yourself float out of it


big beds of bulb kelp were part of our everyday world
>        we all just learned to respect it and let it be
>        there was a give-and-take that we learned
>        living on the shores of a fast-moving pass
that was full of kelp from one end to the other
>        give the kelp its space to live
>        and it would give us food and medicine
>        and feed all the creatures that called it home.

When we were in our young teens back in the early seventies
    we started to notice things changing in our pass and in our bay
the change was gradual but visible to us
    we were raised to always be aware of our surroundings
    because we were all going to be fishermen
    when we were old enough to get our own boats
    these were the things we needed to be aware of
and we knew that things were becoming a little different every year
the huge beds of bulb kelp that we had always taken for granted
    as always being there
    because they had been there since the beginning
    were starting to shrink
more and more every year
    these big kelp beds were shrinking and getting less

and with these huge beds of kelp getting smaller and smaller
    to the point of not existing in Active Pass
also went the homes and food for all the creatures and ourselves
    we were losing our way of life in the pass
    cod got less
    kelp beds got less until we rarely saw any.

What was getting bigger were the BC Ferries getting longer and
    deeper
    they were churning up more of the bottom
    and as they made their daily runs through the pass
    there was more noise more vibration
    also more ferries going through the pass every hour
one ferry was coming and one ferry was going all the time.

We knew the water was getting warmer on the coast
    we were seeing new species coming
    following the warmer water and their feed
with the water getting warmer there were changes
    such as ocean acidification
    changing the natural habitat and natural balance

we watched the migration of California sea lions into our bay and
    Active Pass
    taking over where the kelp beds used to be
    we saw mackerel move onto our coast
    these things did not belong here

as we watched these changes happening
    we also watched the loss of bulb kelp in our pass
we were witnessing the changes that Dad and the old ones said were
    coming.

It has been almost fifty years since I first saw my father's anger
    about what was happening in Active Pass
    and what we were losing in the place we call home.

In these fifty years
    I have had the opportunity to see this coast and all of its beauty
        many times
    it had been a few years since I travelled the coast
    but this year
    I got the opportunity to go back to Prince Rupert for a visit.

Prince Rupert is on Kaien Island
    the airport is on Digby Island five miles to the southwest
    you have to take a ferry between the two islands when you fly
        in
I was so happy to be in a place that I used to know so well
I was overwhelmed by the memories as we landed
    back in a place that holds so many of my family's stories.

As we were disembarking the plane
    there was something seriously missing
    I should have had a strong smell of the ocean
    I should have been overwhelmed by it
but there was nothing.

I felt the heaviness of the loss of the smell
    something so familiar now gone.

As I made my way outside on the ferry I thought
    that I might see the kelp beds up here
    surely we were far enough north that some had survived the
        boats
    and the warming ocean?
I was left feeling the emptiness of something that should have been
    present
    but wasn't
the loss of the smell the loss of the bulb kelp
    washed over me
what used to be and what is today
    it was overwhelming to be hit with these two losses
    back to back.

As I was scanning the water to find even one head of kelp bobbing
    around
    I realized how much we have lost
    I wondered and hoped
that maybe one day our oceans will be home to bulb kelp again.

If the bulb kelp starts returning
    then the smells will come back
    all the creatures that thrive in their homes in the beautiful big
        kelp beds
    will come back
with the return of the bulb kelp also come more
    ling cod rock cod halibut red snappers abalone and otters
    to Active Pass
    to Prince Rupert
to my family and our continuing stories.

I hope that one day my grandchildren will get to see and smell
    some of the things I have shared here.

What will it take?

# Transfearance. Transfearmation.

**ASHLEE CUNSOLO**

---

## i. Transfearance

There is a piece of me that feels broken. Not a big piece. Not a noticeable piece. But a deep piece. One of those pieces that a younger version of me may have revelled in, in the existential angst, and found creativity in the dramatics of the damage of pain.

But not this self.

This self yearns for solace and stillness. For a break from the dull ache of this broken piece. For a moment of reprieve from the enduring feelings of grief and sadness and pain. Or maybe it is fear.

A break from the fear of what is to come. The impending environmental deaths, the coming ecological losses. Fear of an ecological grief without end.

Whatever it is, I'm not sure what to do.

As a good academic, I try to write it. Theorize it. Situate it in historical context. I try to study it, link it to other writers, other thinkers. Try to find where it fits, and give it voice so that I can better understand and know it.

And maybe, just maybe, to make it go away.

It doesn't.

There all the time, it's an uncomfortable companion, implanting itself, and I carry it everywhere. It's like, as Julia Kristeva describes, "the hidden side of my philosophy; its mute sister."

I plant this fear in little places all around me, in the hopes that something more positive than fear can grow. I plant it in my talks, my academic work, my professional roles. I plant it in my actions, my laughter, my tears.

Most of all, I plant it in my writing.

If you look, it's always there.

## ii. Ferality

I spend a lot of my time in the grief of others, who are experiencing a form of ecological suffering related to shifting places, weather, and ecosystems.

For over a decade, I have been immersed in the pain, distress, sadness, anxiety, fear, and anger from people who are at the front lines—who didn't ask to be—in Inuit Nunangat. I have heard stories about the enduring connections that Inuit have to land, generation after generation, in blood, in memory, in culture, in life. And I have worked with people to share these ecological eulogies and elegies, loss and grief through film, stories, photography, research, and writing.

I think about it all the time.

But I don't *think* about it.

And I talk about it all the time.

But I don't *talk* about it.

There is a difference in theorizing about ecological grief and being crippled by it. In articulating it for publication and having it haunt each day. I keep trying to hide from the pain, as though I can outrun it or outresearch it or outwrite it or outmove it. I know that one day, there will be a reckoning.

I know that one day, there will be the moment when I need to look the ecological grief in the eye, face it head-on, open the door.

But not quite yet.

What I am becoming more ready for is the need to share more stories; talk more; bring others together. Clarissa Pinkola Estés writes that "one of the most calming and powerful actions you can do to intervene in a stormy world is to stand up and show your soul."

I am also becoming more certain about breaking free from the constraints of academic work, more certain about finding other ways of expressing stories, voices, wisdom, pain, and sadness, to move beyond my cultivated academic structures. Plant different seeds of ideas from a different stock.

Reclaim intellectual ferality.

### iii. Restoration

I have always been taught, during times of trouble and pain in a stormy world, to go to the land.

To find solace, connection, and healing only the land can give.

Yet, if I'm honest with myself, my current relationship with the land feels somehow abusive. There is love, yes. Deep love. But I'm not reciprocating, not giving back.

I go to the land now when I need something. Go when I am angry. Sad. Hurt. I go when I am stressed, anxious, full of fear. I go to rage, to cry, to ask for help.

I do not ask the land what she needs.

I do not ask how she is.

I do not ask where it hurts.

I cannot bear the truth.

———————

I asked a very wise friend, once, what to do in the face of such rapid changes. How to make sense of the loss of sea ice, the shifting temperatures, the changing plants and animals, the warming oceans, and the wide-scale challenges this poses for so many. He told me that in times like these, we need to love the land. That in times of trouble—in this stormy world—all that we have is our ability to love the land, to give to it what we can, whenever we can, however we can.

A radical love.

A land-based love for resistance and reclamation.

This reminds me of reading an article by Naomi Klein. She describes a moment when she turned to esteemed environmental thinker, writer, and activist Wendell Berry and asked him what to do about the climate crisis. His response? "Stop somewhere, and begin the thousand-year process of knowing that place."

This is difficult for me. I have lived in five different provinces, and many different places. And I have always sought out new landscapes, to immerse myself in the mountains or the rivers, the oceans or the grasslands, of different lands. But I never seem to stay. There's always a moment when I find myself wanting to learn about new places and plants and creatures, when life takes me elsewhere.

But now, in my own grief, I'm trying to stop somewhere, and begin the process of connecting with a particular and rapidly changing place, of getting to know the rhythms and the movements of the land; of seeing how she breathes and responds; how she rests and reciprocates. And I am thinking about this thousand-year process and my responsibilities within this long-after-me relationship.

When you work as a climate change researcher, you are often asked about the past. What did previous epochs look like? How has the temperature fluctuated before? Isn't this all just a natural cycle that has happened before? (To be clear: it is not. We are living in a different time, of rapidly changing, human-induced climate change.) In other words, you spend a lot of time thinking about deep time.

But lately, I've been trying to think about deep futures, about those thousand-year processes that connect us to those who will come after, and pay respects to those who have come before. About the type of time that challenges us all to see ourselves in a relationship with the land that will last well beyond our years. To ground ourselves in place, to fiercely love place, so that maybe others will too.

I'm beginning to think that my work as a climate researcher, and the associated labours of my ecological grief may find its healings in rooting in a place and really getting to know it. In giving back. In learning to listen to the songs and the stories of the living, animate world. In showing gratitude to the animacy and the agency all around me. In noticing the subtle changes, day after day.

In re-envisioning and re-imaging myself differently in relationship to,

in responsibility to,
in responsiveness to,
in radical love with,
the land.

## Notes:

Julia Kristeva, *Black Sun: Depression and Melancholia*, trans. L.S. Roudiez (New York: Columbia University Press, 1989), 4.

Clarissa Pinkola Estés, *Letter to a Young Activist*, 2003, https://localcircles.org /2011/03/10/letter-to-a-young-activist-during-troubled-times-by-clarissa -pinkola-estes/.

Naomi Klein, "The Change Within: The Obstacles We Face Are Not Just External," *The Nation*, May 12, 2014, https://www.thenation.com/article/change-within -obstacles-we-face-are-not-just-external/.

# riparian blues

## BERNARD SOUBRY

---

### i. looking down, clyde river

Where two rivers meet; or rather
where the waters of two languages
go incoherent, babble, feed back
into stream. Where the arc of the
shoreline shortens. You know
in twenty years, so say the maps,
there'll come a rise a forearm's length
to grab up at this place, where once we thought
there were foundations. There are tides,
they say, and then there are *tides*, son.
Some nip at heels and call you names
under the moon across the land's aurora,
sure. But there are those that swallow language,
limb, the years of shoulda started,
gaze up at you from the alluvium
with bared teeth when they smile.

## ii. song for the song of the rose hill kite
(after Don McKay)

There have been other stories and better ones
but here goes: someday soon the Thames
will yawn and stretch and roll right out of bed,
sweep swimmers up from Longbridges to here,
and all the creatures of the sea
and all the creatures of the air
and those without a kayak within reach
will run with it, and you'll regret the time
you tore out floorboards to build shelves, not boats.
Perspective's everything, and from where I'm perched
your saw sounds come up piercing as a call,
and I've been answering; the neighbourhood
moves on. So be it. Sleep as best you can:
from here my voice will keen and cast again,
a net, a tide, a higher kind of mooring.

## iii. onwards, clyde river

Where two rivers meet. Or rather,
where we decided there are two rivers
and what we call meeting: water resonating
from two sources ends up thirdways, cognate
into something else. Sometimes, in order to be the third thing
you must first be two first things: so teach salt tides,
hard tack, water and dried pasta. I looked out
from the shore into the narrows and saw ice
reflecting upwards, flecks of sheet metal
untellable from water, peerless from the sun.

# Where Did We Go Wrong?

## EVELYN C. WHITE

> There is a loneliness that can be rocked. Arms crossed,
> knees drawn up, holding, holding on, this motion, unlike
> a ship's, smooths and contains the rocker. It's an inside
> kind—wrapped tight like skin. Then there is the loneliness
> that roams. No rocking can hold it down. It is alive. On its
> own. A dry and spreading thing.
>
> —Toni Morrison

---

Its once glistening white fur dingy, its countenance despairing, the animal paced back and forth in the blistering heat of about thirty-five degrees. It was thirty years ago that I locked eyes with a polar bear at the Giza Zoo in Cairo, Egypt—nearly seven thousand kilometres from its natural habitat in the Arctic. Indeed, the respected conservation group Polar Bears International reports that 60 percent of *Ursus maritimus* live in Northern Canada.

"This is a disaster," I thought to myself as I stood gazing at the caged creature. Revered as the master of its species in Inuit culture, the captive polar bear soon perished. No surprise there. And as odd as it might sound, the imperilled animal reminded me of an artist then internationally acclaimed for his mastery in the world of entertainment. His name? Michael Joseph Jackson.

Like the King of Pop, I'd grown up in the gritty steel town of Gary, Indiana. As an adoring hometown fan who'd followed his ascent as the lead singer of the Jackson Five (J5), I'd eagerly awaited the release

of Jackson's autobiography, *Moonwalk* (1988), which had been con-
tracted by then New York book editor Jacqueline Kennedy Onassis.

"To many people Michael Jackson seems an elusive personality,
but to those who work with him, he is not," Onassis noted in her fore-
word to the volume. "[His] book provides a startling glimpse of the
artist at work and the artist in reflection."

No longer the brown-skinned, Afro-coiffed, pug-nosed tal-
ent who'd topped the charts with J5 hits such as "ABC" and "I Want
You Back," the singer began altering his appearance, after going
solo, in the 1970s. In the aftermath of the landmark success of his
album *Thriller* (1982), Jackson underwent a radical physical trans-
formation (multiple nose jobs, chin implants, straightened hair,
increasingly alabaster complexion), seemingly aiming to obliterate
his Afrocentric features.

As I watched him receive an award during the 1993 telecast of the
Grammys, it was obvious that the King of Pop had shape-shifted to a
degree that belied his genetic ancestry. Writing in *Moonwalk* about
his adolescence, Jackson had noted that his appearance "began to
depress me....The effect on me was so bad that it messed up my per-
sonality....I believe I'm one of the loneliest people in the world."

Standing at the award show podium, a markedly pale Jackson
elaborated on themes he'd probed in his autobiography. "When you
grow up as I did in front of one hundred million people, since the age
of five, you're automatically different," the singer told the rapt audi-
ence. "My childhood was completely taken away from me."

Shortly after Jackson's unsettling television appearance, I tracked
headline news about a then unprecedented barrage of blizzards, tor-
nadoes, thunder strikes, and hurricane-force winds that ravaged the
Atlantic seaboard from Canada to Honduras. Lamented as an indica-
tor of extreme weather disturbances to come, the ferocious "storm
of the century" led to the deaths of three hundred people and caused
property damage estimated at nearly $7 billion.

Media coverage of the storm's mayhem evoked memories of the distressed polar bear I'd witnessed in the suffocating heat (even by desert standards) of Cairo. "Who in their right mind could even question the reality of climate change?" I thought to myself.

And then came another thought, probably illogical to most but one that held meaning for me as an admirer of the King of Pop, who was increasingly the target of tabloid news: "Why can't the world see that Michael Jackson is in dire trouble?"

Indeed, by the summer of 1993, Jackson was fighting an allegation of child sexual abuse for which he was strip-searched by police and photographed nude. "In an emotional state, Jackson stood on a platform in the middle of the room, took off all his clothes, and the search lasted for approximately 25 minutes," noted a newspaper report. Denying any wrongdoing, Jackson settled the case out of court. A recent documentary, *Leaving Neverland*, re-examines such molestation claims.

A decade later, the singer was arrested on new charges of alleged sexual misconduct with a minor. A heartbreaking mug shot of a ghoulish-looking Jackson, then forty-five, was flashed around the globe. My mind wafted to the wan, anguished, cell-blocked polar bear. Later declared unanimously not guilty on all counts, Jackson nonetheless never recovered from the ordeal. Standing before a crush of reporters on June 25, 2009, a teary-eyed Jermaine Jackson broke the news of his brother's death. Autopsy reports later revealed that Michael Jackson, age fifty, had succumbed to a lethal mix of drugs in his system, notably the surgical anaesthetic propofol, which had been administered to him as a "sleep aid."

After the singer's death, his personal physician had tried, to no avail, to retrieve about forty tubes of prescription skin-whitening cream from Jackson's bedroom. "Michael would not want the world to know about it," ventured the doctor, who was later convicted of involuntary manslaughter and jailed.

For all my youthful adoration of Michael Jackson, I always felt that he was destined for a tragic end. While I revelled in his dazzling performances at local talent shows, I sensed that he was unmoored, unprotected, and exploited. To my mind, the polar bear, the King of Pop, and the climate change now upon us evidence a common denominator: inexcusable inaction in the face of indisputable harm.

This brings me to Jermaine Jackson. Quiet as it's been kept, he stood among those who publicly ridiculed Michael Jackson. "Word to the Badd!!" (1991), the song that Jermaine released in response to his brother's album *Bad* (1987), made reference to Michael Jackson's transformation, the rejection of his heritage, and Jermaine's view that his brother was "too far gone."

A far cry from brotherly love.

As for crying, woefully overlooked in a cascade of smash hits is Michael Jackson's 1995 release "Earth Song." A plea to humanity about the imperilled condition of the planet, the tune's music video includes devastating images of clear-cut forests, drought-parched land, dying wildlife, and violent windstorms.

"Where did we go wrong?" Jackson sings. "Someone tell me why." It was the last song the King of Pop performed, on a Los Angeles rehearsal stage, the night before he died.

## Notes:

Jacqueline Kennedy Onassis, foreword to *Moonwalk* by Michael Jackson (New York: Doubleday, 1988).

*Moonwalk* by Michael Jackson (New York: Doubleday, 1988), p. 96 and p. 162.

Taraborrelli, J. Randy, *Michael Jackson: The Magic and the Madness*, (United Kingdom: Pan MacMillan, 2004).

David Gardner, "Michael Jackson's doctor was 'anxious to retrieve whitening cream from star's bedroom so world would not know about it'," September 28, 2011, https://www.dailymail.co.uk/news/article-2043059/Michael-Jackson-death-trial-Dr-Conrad-Murray-tried-retrieve-whitening-cream.html.

*Michael Jackson Grammy Legend Award 1993*, https://www.youtube.com/watch?v=RPZYBBZQDQO (accessed May 30, 2019).

# Ceremony

**JESSE THISTLE**

---

"What happened here is a tragedy, Earl," Mr. Dobbs, the lead RCMP detective, said to Cree Elder Earl Keshane, eighty years old. Dobbs adjusted his fedora, shook his head, and flipped open his pad of paper to begin the interrogation. The pair stood on Earl's porch, staring at the smouldering embers of the grass fire that'd claimed the lives of three ceremonial fasters of the local Ocean Man Indian reserve.

Dobbs was sent to investigate the July 5, 1937, incident and to arrest Earl, after he was notified by the local Indian agent, Mr. Dunkirk, who knew that the Elder had illegally conducted a fasting ceremony after being forbidden to do so. Earl stood motionless; his deerskin robe and single headdress feather gently blew in the sweltering summer wind. He'd lost two members of his own family. The old man turned to face Dobbs, and a tear rolled down his aged leather cheek—the deep crowfeet wrinkles around his eyes mirrored the prairie landscape: cracked, brown, and starving for water.

"I have been doing these ceremonies all my life," Earl said, his voice warbling a bit. He steadied himself and eased into his rocking chair. "Please, sit, sit." He motioned to Dobbs to take the chair next to him. The detective did so and placed his trench coat on a nail jutting out of the cabin siding.

Earl went on, "Nothing like this has ever happened." He bowed his head and ran his hands over his long white braids, searching the wooden planks beneath his feet for words.

"Earl," said Dobbs, "I've known you all my life—remember when you'd bounce me on your knee when Momma got tired?" Dobbs reached over and rubbed the Elder's leg. "You ranched with my grandpappy and dad; so did your sons. Always were good farmhands. Just explain to me what happened."

Comforted somewhat, Earl leaned back and remembered back to when the land around Yellow Grass, Saskatchewan, was green and filled with herds of wild bison and lush grass, years before his family worked for white people like the Dobbses. Back then, fasting ceremonies were conducted regularly. They helped his people make relations with the land, all its creatures, all its relatives, and with the living and non-living forces of the world. A longing for that time panged in his heart as he began to recount the tragedy.

"I'm eighty now," Earl began. "And when I was a young man, before the treaty signings, I was taken into ceremony, like the one yesterday." The old man shifted his feet as his hand searched the wall for his cane. He found it resting near the door. "I was given a traditional name; I am sorry I can't share it with you—protocol forbids it—but it came with the job of teaching others how to sit with the silence of the land. We do that by fasting."

Dobbs followed along, making notes on his pad, a bead of sweat upon his brow.

"And every ten years," Earl continued, "I take our future leaders out and teach them our ways. That's what I was doing here." Earl waved his hand over the land out toward the area where the fasters were consumed by the midnight blaze. The only thing that stood on the open plain were the half-scorched staffs the fasters had planted outside their lodges to mark the four directions. A few blackened tobacco ties and feathers still hung off them. It was an eerie sight.

"I took everyone into the Sweat Lodge at six yesterday evening and had my nephew, sixteen, minding the hot rocks and fire and the water when I called for it." Earl made a motion with his hands like he was forking up grandfather stones with a set of antlers inside the Sweat Lodge, like he, as the ceremonial conductor, would do. It was a job Earl was known for around these parts, a job that had been illegal for forty years since the passing of the Potlatch laws banning Indian ceremonies in Canada. Earl looked at Dobbs and cowered, afraid that he was incriminating his nephew.

"Don't worry," Dobbs assured him. "We just need to get to the bottom of this—we can leave your nephew out of it. Dunkirk will not find out."

The old man's brow eased and he regained his train of thought. "We took them out on the land and into their individual lodges at nine," he went on. "Right before the sun set. That's how we count the days. Then we went to bed."

Dobbs flipped the page and scribbled down the time, careful to note every detail. The dry Saskatchewan wind picked up and knocked his fedora off his head, sending it tumbling across the porch. Earl jutted his cane out with the speed of a lynx and caught it before it took flight.

"You see," Earl said. "Gotta be careful. These winds ain't like before." He smacked his lips as if tasting the moisture in the air; he flipped the hat back to Mr. Dobbs. The detective was astonished the old man could move that fast.

"The rain, too. It's different." Earl stuck his hand out as if to catch a raindrop. He clutched his fingers into a fist and shook it, a look of anger across his face.

"I remember when I was a boy." Earl leaned over toward the detective, the cool steel of ice in his eyes. "I went out hunting buffalo with my grandfather—he was a Chief. The rain used to come all the time." He gripped the arms of his rocking chair; his fingers were powerful like eagle claws and made the wood moan. "The grasses were once lush—never any dust or drought." He stopped and corrected himself. "Well, not exactly; there was the occasional drought, but not like this." The old man peered off into the distance at the cloud of approaching dust rolling over the horizon.

Dobbs watched it too and remembered that when he was a little boy with Earl on his father's land, the undulations of the prairie weren't as menacing as the last eight Depression years were in South Saskatchewan. Dust storms and death had become common occurrences for white farmers and Natives alike.

"Your people did this," Earl said, the chair still squeaking under his grip. "It's because of what you did." He rocked back and forth, the creak of the floorboards complaining underneath his weight and movement.

Dobbs cocked his head. "How so?" he asked, his pen now dormant on the pad.

"Those bison were murdered. It was them who tamped down the grass, ate it up and shit it back out—that held in the moisture. Plus, all the birds and insects that lived with the bison—they reseeded the grass every season and it held the soil down; they had a role to play too. Like, um, it's...what's the word..." Earl scratched his chin, searching the ancient thesaurus that was his brain.

"An environment?" Dobbs offered.

"Yeah, that's it, but we Indians just call that 'relatives.'" Earl rocked, the creaks the only noises between them. He tried to say something more but tears chocked back his throat. Dobbs tried to refocus on the investigation.

"Earl, please, the fire—"

"No!" Earl shouted, a firmness in his voice like he'd been interrupted by a child. "You listen to me, goddamn it." He rapped his gnarled cane on the porch and asserted his authority. "It's important, what I'm saying."

Dobbs recoiled, respectful of the man who'd helped raise him years ago.

"Those farmers came and ripped this land to all Christ. Planting all kinda stuff that don't belong. That's what caused the droughts and the dust." A heat radiated behind Earl's rage; his octogenarian body quaked with raw emotion.

"That's what I was trying to fix with the ceremony—to get our young to make relatives with the prairie again and ask the animals back to fix this disaster." Earl's eyes were big as he took a deep breath and exhaled.

"Oh, I see," Dobbs said, his pen now active again. "So, you were aware of the aridness and the potential for fire? Yesterday was the hottest day on record—114 degrees. Hottest day ever in Canada."

"Of course I knew. I know this land better than anyone." Earl stood up and pointed to the burnt-out lodges and then over to the rock pit where the fire for the Sweat Lodge was.

"And we took every precaution to put the fire out. See."

All Dobbs could see was a pile of dirt, two feet high and three feet across.

"That's where the fire was. We buried it. And we fasted alongside them in the cabin here, so we did no cooking, had no fire after the Sweat Lodge closed. Just went to sleep."

Dobbs scribbled more notes as a jet-black 1932 Oldsmobile came barrelling up the driveway from up over the horizon. It sent a plume of dust into the air fifty feet high and three hundred feet long. It was Dunkirk. He had four high-ranking RCMP with him. Dunkirk jumped out and ran up to the porch, his finger extended and accusatory.

"That's the man!" he yelled. "He's the one who caused the fire. Arrest him."

"But we don't know that for sure," Dobbs protested as he tried to get in between Earl and the officers.

"No!" Dunkirk yelled, cutting off Dobbs. "I forbade him to do any Indian ceremonies yesterday and he did it anyways. Now three people are dead."

The officers pushed Dobbs aside and wrestled the old man to the ground, then cuffed him. The force of it was uncalled for—Earl didn't resist in the slightest.

The four large Mounties muscled Earl forward with his hands bound behind his back, then pushed his head into the car as if he were a common criminal. Earl stared out the back-seat side window at the ceremonial staffs that blew in the distance, then over at Dobbs.

Dobbs's eyes locked on Earl's. "You can't just arrest him like that. I haven't finished my investigation."

"Yes, we can," Dunkirk fired back. "I'm the agent and I knew you'd be too close to Earl to arrest him." Dobbs wanted to punch Dunkirk right in the mouth for treating his old friend the way he did.

"Yeah? How?"

"I knew he'd go ahead with his voodoo magic after I told him not to, so I came out here on horseback last night after the sun went down and I seen all these lodges and the lights out in the cabin."

Dobbs turned his head out toward where the fasters had been consumed by fire, and he walked past Dunkirk to get a better look at the pile of dirt to see if there was any chance of the embers escaping.

*Nope,* he thought. *The old man made sure. No fire could spread from there.*

Just then, he smelled another waft of smoke but it was different, familiar almost, and he realized Dunkirk was right behind him.

"Damn shame," Dunkirk said, smacking his suspenders, "these Indians dying like that, but the law is the law, and he's got to pay for what he's done."

Dobbs turned, saw a cigarette hanging out of Dunkirk's mouth.

It all clicked into place.

# Short Walk Home

**REBECCAH NELEMS**

---

What is it called when you look down and see, in the pores of your skin, trees on a steep hill, returning to the earth amidst branches reaching up to receive and distribute sunlight? What is the name for it, when your hand shows you salmon spawning, baring their bones in fossilite form? What is the English word for when the veins rushing across your feet are the ice cracking in spring? For when your home fills with the tall firs that gave it form, needles scratching your cheek as you make your way into the next room? Remembering?

As a child, I went with my dad to X̱aaydaga Gwaay.yaay (Haida Gwaii), where we visited a former X̱aayda village. There were no buildings anymore, no totems to look up at; their remains were indistinguishable from the earth. In the mist and damp of the forest on that spring morning, a X̱aayda guide gifted us stories. Not only did the ancestors have stories to tell, he said: the land, trees, and animals also remember. These were the stories of "All Our Relations." He spoke of the wolf, saying that in X̱aayda traditions, the wolf is the land-bound equivalent of the killer whale, representing humility, loyalty, bravery, and kinship. I watched my father as he stood in his smallness receiving each story, word, and silence.

The moment I learned of my father's death, I gasped so deeply for air that a spirit dived deep into my lungs. I stood on the road in front of my house, stunned, and every cell in me began to morph. If he hadn't taught me how the lungs work, how oxygen moves through them and then into the blood, into every crevice of your body, I might've missed it. He knew what he was doing.

Once I stood in the viewing gallery of an operating room in the middle of the night, watching him conduct a double lung and heart transplant. I didn't anticipate the sacredness of that draped and sterile other world of his: families in the moment of losing their kin giving life to another family; nurses and doctors with only eyes showing, reverently holding both recently deceased and fighting-for-life organs; the gentle, soft, dark cave of a chest cavity exposed; tubes and machines tenderly breathing and beating a man's heart for him. No one ever tells you you can live through your heart being taken out of your body. But you can.

He came to me in my dreams the night after he died in response to my plea: How could I ever sleep again only to wake to his absence? Holding out a cup of tea for me to drink, he said nothing, but exuded profound peace. The tea's golden colour was mesmerizing, but it was the intoxicating scent of honey that lingered long after I awoke, my nostrils incredulous. I've never had a sense of smell.

When a tree dies, it doesn't fold back into the earth immediately. It stays standing, or lying, holding its place in a forest or landscape, sometimes for years. In fact, it is in this moment of death that a tree gives the most life it ever will. It becomes home to more insects than ever before, which in turn nourish the birds, bats, and small mammals, the creatures who bury nuts or poop out seeds that become new trees and plants, before the animals themselves become the food for larger mammals.

What if a person dying is no different from a tree folding back into the earth? For far longer than Western societies have proclaimed and enforced their "laws of the land," countless Indigenous traditions have told us there is no higher law than that of the earth. How is it that the English language permits us to speak of "nature" and "land" as if we ourselves are not nature and of the land? Einstein named this grand forgetting the "optical delusion of consciousness," the belief that we are free-floating, detached, and separate beings. How do some people imagine we might reconcile ourselves with the earth the same way we are destroying it: "managing" and "mitigating" the "effects" of climate change? Is not the challenge similar to the one acutely experienced in the loss of a beloved? How do you restore yourself to a sense of wholeness when it feels like part of you is forever missing?

There is the kind of change that happens when a tree dies. It is the continual regeneration of every cell of your being, the changing of the guard every millimoment of every day. It is the falling fallow of the field, the wasp transfigured into the fig, the compost joining the earth so new life can be born. In the infinite regeneration of life itself, birth and death, giving and receiving, are intimately inseparable. This is the *virtuous* cycle of life of which BC political philosopher Jim Tully writes. And then there is the kind of change that happens when this cycle is forgotten, when abundance is converted into scarcity and is not and never enough, when one species systematically and on a grand scale thwarts the life of all. This hierarchical world, for Tully, is the *vicious* cycle.

The virtuous and vicious cycles tell stories that have very different morals and endings. There is power in every story, as Cherokee-German-Greek author Thomas King reminds us, for, once told, a story can never be unheard. But the most dangerous stories are the ones that tell us they are the only story, that there is no other possible ending: the *just how it is* stories. These stories become the stilted air we breathe, the closed vats we bathe in, the silent tyranny of the taken for granted and assumed. These stories viciously silence the *it can be otherwise* and *it is already otherwise* stories.

My dad was known as a trailblazer. I often thought of him, rather, as a bit reckless: like when he jumped onto the icy pond to test if it was frozen (it wasn't); when he would steer with his knee while drinking coffee, shifting gears, and telling you a story with his hands; or when he took young children into the wilderness for days without food because we were going to catch fish (we did not). The bravest thing he ever did was come into a world of violence, suffering, withheld love, and alienated privilege, and decide with every fibre of his being to refuse to believe the stories he was told. He simply lived otherwise, and told everyone who would listen a story of love and connection: with his eyes, his words, and his hands. It is this bravery we need in these climate-changing times, not the hero's rescue. It is the only bravery we have ever needed.

A relation came to me in the garden in the weeks after my dad's death. So close did he hum, he needed no name. But he'd not have needed one anyway; we'd worked alongside one another in the garden for some time. (If the exchange of wild strawberries, nectar, dirt in skin crevices, pollen, water, and the blush of blooms doesn't make you friends, I'm not sure what does.) He hovered long and so near that his swift wings blew my hair back. This was no social visit. My dad had filled the hummingbird feeders right before he died. I closed my eyes and received his most tender of gifts: his swift wings so my skin could feel, his breeze into my rawness, his ease into my ache. Weight of being for being: I recalled the lightness of my dad's ashes as I carried them out of the funeral home.

Passionate about birds, my dad had a beautiful collection of found feathers. Since he's passed, I find feathers everywhere. They mix with flakes of skin, pollen, and moth wings that sweep across the fir trees of my home. They fill my lungs, my line of vision. There's one on my keyboard right now; no, there are two, three. It's like my dad's little joke. He never *could* stop retelling his own jokes.

Since he's passed, the only stories I hear are stories of the earth, told by the trees, plants, and birds. These are stories without heroes, and instead with tangled webs of characters from the stars to the mosses, none of whom need development, all of whom have a role. Stories without nouns, only verbs. Stories of rifts but no exile, that speak in poetry, not philosophy. Stories of remembering how short the walk home really is: with a mere turning of the head, a breeze from elsewhere touches your neck, and the world reappears.

## Notes:

James Tully, "Deparochializing Political Theory and Beyond: A Dialogue Approach to Comparative Political Thought," *Journal of World Philosophies* 1, no. 1 (2016): 61.

Thomas King, *The Truth About Stories: A Native Narrative* (Toronto: House of Anansi Press, 2003), 10.

# Absence

**ELYSIA FRENCH**

I'm sitting in my sister's backyard, which seems impossibly green, admiring the fullness of the hostas and hydrangeas that line the fence. My niece, Ev, is lying in the grass, pensively picking a bouquet of clover and dandelion. Their yard is just south of Lake Ontario. Together, Ev and I agree, we can smell the subtleties of the shoreline. The cardinal she calls Reddy flies overhead, a squirrel scampers across the lawn, and her dog barks. Ev is six and happiest here in her backyard. The sweetness of a warm summer breeze moves through the leaves of her favourite oak tree.

"Auntie, do you think the wind is music for the trees to dance?"

For Ev, this observation about the poetry of the natural world is not exceptional. She has a profound attentiveness to her non-human surroundings. She is a literal tree hugger. She removes snails from sidewalks, sings with cicadas, collects magical rocks, leaves food for ants. She protects her yard's lone chrysalis, patiently waiting for a butterfly (or moth) to emerge.

Ev's care and curiosity also have their limits. A wasp stung her when she was five, and from then on she developed a deep fear of animals with stingers. On more than one occasion, I've watched her run in terror from the sound of the buzzing bee.

Today, however, I see something shift. As Ev skips into the house to get a drink of water, she notices a dead honeybee on the back-yard patio. The delicate insect lies on the ground, on her back, her wings peacefully tucked beneath her body. Her antennae, legs, and abdomen are curled slightly inward and upward as though she is taking a rest. Her stinger is intact and her pollen combs remain dry, empty, and unfulfilled, not unlike the preserved specimens mounted, categorized, framed, and displayed in a natural history museum.

For Ev, the bee is a tiny, stinging predator. For me, the bee is an integral part of my sister's backyard ecosystem, if one with an ambivalent history. Despite Ev's and my divergent understandings and experiences, we sit together, quietly watching the bee, as if it might turn over and take flight at any moment. After a long time, Ev turns and asks:

"Auntie, how did the bee die?"

I pause, searching for an appropriate answer: Pesticides? Colony collapse disorder? Infection? But the answer does not come.

We decide to move the bee to a more appropriate final resting place. Gently, I pick up the bee and place her in Ev's cupped hands. Ev walks over to the fence, kneels in the grass, and softly places the bee in the soil beneath the hydrangeas.

"Do you think the bee had a family?" Ev pushes on.

"Yes," I answer, "I believe the bee had a very big family."

---

What did the death of this singular bee mean for her colony and for the interconnected human and non-human networks it supported? For Ev, this encounter opened the possibility of knowing another species and altered her relationship to honeybees: they do more than sting. For me, the delicate body of this tiny being prompted an unexpected emotional response. Even though I did not know why the bee had died, her death reminded me, viscerally, of the uneasiness, anger, and sadness I feel in the face of climate change. Ev's curious and thoughtful spirit drew my attention to the dead bee; would I have even noticed her delicate body on the patio? But the bee's death struck a sensitive chord in me: I was reopened to an awareness of the crucial and intricate human-non-human relationships currently in need of care if there is to be any chance of slowing climate change. In that moment, the bee embodied the global climatic loss of life taking place, but, perhaps more importantly, presented a space for me to experience and feel this loss locally.

Increasingly, I witness rallying support for honeybees, which are promoted as essential pollinators, especially for farmers. However, even as we mourn their present and future absence, we must bear in mind the troubling history of the honeybee's existence. Honeybees are a non-native species here in Canada that, in the view of many researchers, has colonized habitats from native pollinators. In other words, the currently publicized absence of honeybees already obscures the ongoing legacies of colonialism that are evident in the quietly absent native pollinators. If we look to honeybees for assistance in the face of the enormity of climate change, then what does it mean that we look to an animal that is so thoroughly implicated in settler agriculture?

Lingering with the stillness of the bee, I took the opportunity to think about the slow and measured connections between human and non-human life. I contemplated whether climate change, as a potentially catastrophic event in our larger story of shared multispecies relationships, insists upon greater communication and empathy between species. The body of this honeybee invited me to think about climate change on an intimate and local level: it was an indication of environmental transformation that I felt emotionally, physically, and intellectually. The remains of the bee pointed toward my own negligence. I realized that my ordinary interactions with non-human species often render them invisible; they become so familiar that I can neglect their existence and my daily experiences with them. A poignant encounter (such as the one with the bee) can remind us that our non-human counterparts are always, although perhaps not permanently, present, even when a deep understanding of our relationship with them may be absent.

Absence is an unmistakable and urgent sign of climate change: what is not here, now, that once was, and what is here, now, that likely will not be in the future. But absence is not always stark, not always an absolute void. Consider the backyard honeybee, a "bad tick season," or the spread of wild parsnip. What has occurred in our environment to create favourable conditions for these species, and what is absent for them to be present? What presences might hasten, in turn, their absence? Colony collapse disorder currently threatens the honeybee, and in turn, the honeybee continues to displace native pollinators such as the bumblebee. Absence may mean extinction, but it may also look like my sister's backyard: the honeybees, the hostas, and the hydrangeas represent an entangled ecosystem that includes the healthy, the invasive, the displaced, the missing, the invisible, the depleting, and the dying.

The moment with the honeybee reminded me to stay attuned to the full range of absences taking place in "our own backyards." Absence, as an entangled system, reminds us that mundane non-human relationships are as important as, and often inseparable from, the rare and remarkable ones. When I think about climate change, I too often conjure the haunting image of stranded and displaced polar bears, coupled with the unsettling screeches, splashes, trickles, and cracks of melting glacial ice and rising sea levels. Although this now iconic imagery belies an intimate, difficult, and lived reality for northern communities, the backyard honeybee showed me that we must also pay attention to the changes, the emptiness, and the absences occurring in our own, southern backyards.

The non-human world is speaking to us. The bee, of course, is just one representative of a multitude of species calling out for care, even if that care is complicated. In listening to these voices, we come to know and feel climate change in the gentle intimacies of noticing local absence. Whether recognizing vulnerability or invasiveness, endangerment or abundance, staying attuned to local multispecies relationships opens space for experience, storytelling, and building care.

––––––––––

I am not sure if Ev ever finds herself thinking about the backyard honeybee, but I often do.

We recently returned to her impossibly green backyard to play hide-and-seek among the overgrown hostas. We again encountered a bee. This time, the bee (very much alive) softly hovered above Ev's head. I watched Ev freeze anxiously at the sound of a circling bee, instead of instantly running in fear.

Ev's fear still exists, but I believe the other honeybee played an important role in her response. The dead bee, and the family she left behind, introduced Ev to kinship. Instead of looking away, we took the opportunity to lean into an experience of absence: to spend time with it, to witness the emptiness, and to build care. The honeybee's death and burial offered an opportunity to introduce and rethink the story of shared lives in a backyard ecosystem, which serves as a microcosm for the global climatic crisis. The bee became a tool to communicate everyday encounters with climate change by making visible the fragility of multispecies relationships. The honeybee was present in my sister's backyard, in part, because of environmental absence; still, Ev and I mourned the loss of the bee. This complex intimacy of absence underscores the importance of being attentive to what is present, what is absent, and what may and can return.

# Underfolk

**DAVID HUEBERT**

Mum asked what I wanted to be for Halloween and I told her one of the underfolk, the creatures who live in the tidal flats. We were walking around the waterfront and there was a cruise ship pulling in, a big white top hat on the black still sea.

"Underfolk?"

"Yeah."

"What are they?"

"Sea creatures, sort of. Amphibians. They're like household sprites, but with tongues made of seaweed and barnacle eyes."

"Household sprites?"

"Yeah, sprites. You know, like gnomes. But helpful."

"Well. Seaweed and barnacle eyes. Very imaginative. Where'd you learn about these underfolk?"

"Sam told me about them."

Mum frowned. It was a frown I knew well. A frown related to Sam. A frown that meant she thought I was acting "troubled" again, that she wore when Mr. Humphries said I was still in the denial phase.

We left it at that. Stood together looking up at the cruise ship. Seventeen storeys of white and on top a climbing wall and a crane with a viewing bubble and a big green inflatable giraffe. In the summer the cruise ships come and go and the locals sell them fish and chips, beads, and bracelets. I've often wondered what it's like to be that high out over the ocean. So high up you can't even see the waves anymore, just the flat endless blue. Sam and I used to talk about climbing up the balconies and stowing away on board.

Harbour Street was full of women tanned bright orange, men in colourful shirts and white running shoes. It was high tide, as it had to be for the cruise ships to come in. On the other side of the harbour, tankers were picking up payloads from the refineries. We stood at the railing and Mum spoke toward the ocean.

"So how serious are you, about dressing up as an underfolk?"

"There's no known singular for the word 'folk.'"

She grinned, and meant it. "That's my little Dictionary."

"I just say 'an underperson.'"

"Couldn't you just be a TV again? We still have the costume. Or remember last year, when you were Garth and Sam was Wayne?"

I watched Mum realize she'd made a mistake. A foghorn sounded in the distance, and we stood holding the guardrail and staring out over the black sea. A pop bottle bobbed against the jetty, kissed a cube of Styrofoam. Mum once told me she used to see seals and porpoises in the harbour, but I'd never seen anything but trash and seagulls and diesel rainbows.

"Maybe I'll just stay home."

Mum sucked her teeth. A tanker slumped across the calm harbour, slid through the breakwater and on through the blameless black.

---

Sam had just been diagnosed the night he told me about the underfolk. We'd biked down to our spot—a little cave nestled into a cliff, the slab of the walkway jutting overhead. Sometimes we would take our bikes over the hill and into the refinery through the train tracks. If Mum was on night shift, she'd be in the alkylation unit, and we'd ride up to the fence next to the rusted-out Do Not Enter signs and imagine her climbing the stacks to inspect the gauges and pipelines. Mum said it wasn't glamorous but she was responsible for a lot of lives. She had to wear coveralls and no matter how much she showered and did laundry she said she still smelled the oil in her hair and on her clothes.

So sometimes we biked around but mostly we just sat there and talked. We liked watching the refinery lights at night. Even though they're toxic they're the most beautiful thing in the world at night, glimmering off the harbour water or the flats.

It was hard being at the spot when Sam was sick, even if he didn't really have any symptoms. The doctors had said he shouldn't push it too hard, that there was a chance of him getting confused or getting lost again. Sam was the opposite of sick—all smiles and promises. But I could see that he was sad. He wasn't ready to leave, and I wasn't either. With Mum I was always "precocious" or "gifted." With Sam I was just me—a little nerdy, a little gassy, maker of seismic snores. He called me Pipsqueak or the Calculator or Snora Pakora, but there was nothing mean about it.

I didn't have much to say that night and I guess he could tell the diagnosis was weighing on me, because he asked if I was all right and I cried. Just a little, which was so stupid and unfair because I didn't want to make it about me.

He grabbed my shoulder. "It's all right," he said. "I'm still the big brother. And I always will be." And then he was sniffling too, refinery lights gleaming in the corner of his eye.

Then I blurted out a stupid question. I knew the answer but I asked it anyway: "Will we ever see each other again?"

"Yes," he said, totally confident. Sam usually didn't talk about heaven or anything like that, so I stared back at him, not following. "Don't worry," he said. "I'm not going far." I kept staring, so he pointed down to the tidal flats, asked if I'd heard of the underfolk. I said no, so he told me about them. Creatures that lived in the sand, too small for the human eye to register. He told me about the barnacle eyes and seaweed tongues, said they fed off microscopic life forms. He said they always spoke in doubled words, like "It was warm-warm, and wet-wet." During the day they came up into people's houses and they did small, secret things to make them feel better. Like replacing the toilet paper or installing updates on their computers. And he told me they were in the refinery too. That they were doing their best to help the workers with maintenance, what with Streamline wanting to do the bare minimum. They wanted to help keep the harbour clean. But right now they were sick. Maybe they were sick because the harbour was.

After all this, he looked over at me, completely serious, and said that in a way he was looking forward to becoming an underperson. "Weird, right?"

I shrugged. "Not that weird." You don't tell your terminally ill brother when he's talking crazy. "All they do is good things. They make people happy. I can believe it." I wanted to.

Sam smiled, showed his big front teeth.

A fifteen-foot flare shot up out of the refinery and he jumped up and pointed at it, nearly smacking his head on the overhang. "There!" he shouted. "That's them. That's their torch. That's how they send signals to the other underfolk in different harbours."

For a moment I thought he'd gone full bats. But he looked so sure I had to trust him.

I reached up and tugged on his septum ring and he shot back, hands on his face, screaming: "Ow, oh no, my nose, my nose! It's been defenestrated!"

I laughed and sniffled and wiped my eyes, knowing I was too old for this and not caring. "That's not what 'defenestrated' means," I told him, cackling. When my smile faded I realized that I felt a little better, and that he had been right: he was still my big brother and always would be. We stayed there for a long time, watching the lights throb and shudder in the flats and thinking about all the creatures living down there, too small for the eye to see.

Mr. Humphries pushed his glasses all the way up his nose, which I'd started thinking was some sort of code. Then he asked what my plans were for Halloween. I told him I thought I'd stay home, that I might be too old to trick-or-treat.

"At twelve?"

What was I supposed to say? "Yes. I am twelve."

Somehow, the glasses kept going up. "I know you're still working through the denial stage, and I'm proud of your progress. But at times like these it's important to try to cultivate joy. Social rituals can help us move on."

When Mum had said I needed to talk to someone, I knew what she meant. Talking to "someone" never means talking to someone you like. Talking to "someone" means talking to someone who takes notes and uses terms like "processing" and "companioning." And maybe you get what they're trying to do but you just don't like it because you're not ready to move on. Maybe all you want is to see Sam, talk to him, tug on his septum ring and have him pretend you ripped his nose off.

The floor in Mr. Humphries's office was laminate hardwood. Like a stomped-on world of Jenga. I stared deep into it, willing an underperson to appear. No luck. The clock said one more minute.

"Can I go?"

"Promise me you'll think about it."

"Promise. Can I go?"

Mr. Humphries took his glasses off and wiped them, which I took as code for yes. Outside, the air was thick and salty, and it was nice to be alone. Rotting leaves whispered under my shoes as I walked home for nut loaf and Brussels sprouts.

After dinner I rode down to the spot alone. Mr. Humphries had told me this was not a good idea, but right then I didn't want good ideas. I wanted the quiet of the harbour, the memory of Sam's septum ring catching the street lamps as he hopped a curb on his BMX. It was already dusk when I got there. Mum was on nights so it didn't much matter how long I sat there thinking about the underfolk and looking back and forth between the flats and the photo on my home screen—a selfie Sam took of him and me at the spot, the ocean peeled back to reveal the wet sand and a mountain of seaweed, refinery stacks like the lairs of robot supervillains. As I looked at it, I wished I could crawl into the tidal flats myself, submit to the salty cool.

The tide was almost halfway in. The thing about the tide is it's asymmetrical. Twice a day the sea peels back like a great wide lip, but it's never the same two times. Sam used to say it was the asymmetry that made it beautiful. He said that most people saw symmetry as perfection, in faces and architecture and the world. But Sam said the way he made his drawings and photographs appealing was by putting everything just a little off-centre. "Crookedness is interesting," he had said. I couldn't think of anything more interesting than Sam's photographs and drawings. He had one triptych of photographs he'd taken of the refineries during sunsets, flares towering over the drums, the stacks rising up like rusty busted fence posts. Like ladders to another world where no one would want to be. A dark and jagged beauty that only Sam could have seen and brought to life. Mum had them up in the kitchen, and sometimes after breakfast I'd stare into the depths of them, the way you'd stare into the embers of a campfire.

I gazed out to the refinery, lights slurring off the tidal flats. I thought about Mum on her panel in the alkylation unit, drinking coffee after coffee but never really waking up. A large flare shot up and I watched it burn, remembering what Sam had said about underfolk messages. The gas was maybe ten feet high and it was shooting out a little crooked, like a bent Roman candle. I wondered if there was someone else watching it somewhere. Maybe someone tiny, with barnacle eyes and a seaweed tongue. I wondered if such a creature could tell me what the torch meant, if it meant anything at all. The flare slanted and sputtered and hissed away. Like a snake retracting into the shadows.

**Note:**
This story is excerpted from *Sick Harbour*, a novel-in-progress.

# Bluestem & Bull Kelp

**BETSY WARLAND**

---

## i. Tallgrass & Tall Ships

There are three things I know about my settler great-grandfather.

Thing One: he immigrated to the US Midwest from Norway in the mid-1800s.

Thing Two: as an old man, his hearing was so poor that my mother and her sisters would hide beneath his bed and giggle at his voluminous farts before he fell asleep.

Thing Three: as a young child, I overheard my aunts recalling how, in his old age, my great-grandfather's greatest pleasure was to walk down to the river two miles away and "fish with the Indians." In the early 1950s, this seemed fantastical to me as the only Indians that I knew existed were in westerns on TV. In that part of the Midwest, it would be a couple of decades before the Sauk, Sioux, and Fox histories, and the devastating Black Hawk War and Treaty in 1832, resurfaced as subjects of relevance for settler scholars.

During my childhood, I also overheard a passing comment in my uncles' post-dinner conversation that the Midwest had been a sea of three-to-ten-foot-high bluestem tallgrass when great-grandpa arrived. This image provoked a strange euphoria and vertigo in me. The image of a sea of tallgrass—contrasted to the endless grid of one-mile-square sections mechanically plowed, seeded, cultivated, fertilized, sprayed with pesticides and herbicides, then harvested—was unrecognizable. When the tallgrass vanished, so did settler memory of it. In Native American memory, it remained intrinsic.

## ii. Bluestem Tallgrass

Sway of the tallship my great-grandfather sailed the Atlantic on.
Sway of the tallgrass that he eradicated.

Found mini-essay (*Roget's Thesaurus*):
**sway**
*power*, 160.
*influence*, 178.
*oscillate*, 317.
*be irresolute*, 601.
*motive*, 612.
*governance*, 733.

**Power**: n. superiority, omnipotence, exertion, control.

**Influence**: n. upper hand, climate, knowing the right people, rule.

~~~~~~~~~tallgrass sway~~~~~~~~~

**Oscillate**: v. undulate, wave, swing, move to and fro.

Cross-Atlantic sailing. My great-grandfather fleeing yet another famine. Then, his journey halfway across the hundred-million-hectare swath of tallgrass swaying from Southern Manitoba to the Gulf of Mexico; from Wisconsin to Oklahoma.

Bluestem that had flourished for ten thousand years.

**Be irresolute**: v. be of two minds, change sides.

Did he ever have second thoughts? Waver about his actions? Within seventy years, the bluestem was burned. Plowed under by settlers rendering Native American inhabitants and wildlife homeless.

**Motive**: n. propaganda, pressure, hard sell, promises.

Indigenous people resisted. The Black Hawk War resulted in brutal treatment and the Black Hawk Treaty of 1832 sealed the opening of the tallgrass prairies for unlimited settlement.

70 years = 100 million hectares of tallgrass gone.

Our settler mindset: we demand ever-increasingly rapid technological change yet insist climate change will advance slowly.

## iii. Bull Kelp

My love of bull kelp (and its sinuous movement) prompted me to write this essay; prompted me to find out more about the tallgrass and recognize sway is in my DNA. For Salish Sea Indigenous people, like Rosemary Georgeson, kelp has remained vital.

1981. I migrated to the West Coast. Vancouver's surrounding landscape was so reminiscent of Norway's mountains, forests, islands, and sea. It was then I began coming to Galiano; became friends with Galiano residents and authors Jane Rule and Dorothy Livesay.

It was Galiano that taught me island. Instructed me in what island is when rooted in sea. Galiano's abundant bull kelp mesmerized me with its undulating sway, its anchoring holdfast, elegant stipe, its pneumatocyst carbon-monoxide-filled bladder float sprouting many-bladed long-long arms elegant and lyrical as Matisse's naked women circle-dancing in *La Danse*. And its taste? Addictive! And nutritious.

The Hermetic saying "As above, so below" embodies the land and underwater bull kelp forests of Galiano. Both forests harbour a vast array of life, as did the bluestem's dynamic ecosystem of insects, small mammals, birds, bison, elk, deer, and the Native Americans who thrived among them. On Galiano, the thriving bull kelp forests have almost disappeared in the wake of ever-increasing tanker traffic, ferry, tourist expedition, and sport-fishing powerboat traffic compounded by increased industrial waste, acidification, and the lethal effect on marine life due to ocean warming.

*Governance:* n. divine right, lawful authority, white supremacy, seizure of power, rule of terror.

~~~~~~~~*bull kelp sway & swirl*~~~~~~~~

*Sway:* v. influence, have the ear of.

In utero, hearing is our first sense to develop, and in death, our last to leave us.

This brings me to the crucial link between us humans and the rest of the inhabitants in our natural world: our basic need for tenderness.

In the absence of an abiding tenderness, research and policy change will inevitably be inadequate, easily circumvented, and perfunctory. Prosperity will remain our rudder.

Compounding this is that within the span of just two hundred years, North Americans' place of residency has flipped from being 90 percent rural to almost 90 percent urban. As a result—on a daily basis—our experience of nature is minimal and so taken for granted that we find ourselves saying: "It looks fine to me."

A couple of summers ago, during a long drought in Vancouver, plants, scrubs, trees were slowly but obviously dying. Few residents even noticed. Even fewer came to their rescue. Now, as in Cape Town—the first city of the world to be running out of water—nature reminds us we are in fact not in control.

*Tender:* ten-, to stretch, tendril.

As it becomes more and more apparent that old knowledges of Indigenous Peoples are invaluable. History has proven how rapidly and radically we can change nature. Now, we must rapidly and radically change ourselves.

# Love and Lifeboating

**KYO MACLEAR**

---

In the wake of my father's progressive dementia, amid his daily efforts to stay afloat, I bound myself to his unmooring, made common cause with his vulnerability. I witnessed the breakdown of navigational systems. I saw night become day. I witnessed seasons flip. December became March. June became October. He took to wearing a heavy woollen scarf in summer. White tennis shoes in the dead of winter. My father bellwethered climate change.

Sundown is when language falters. Cared for in our home on weekends, my father quietened at nightfall, I noticed. My sons learned the gift of affiliating with his non-speaking presence. There were hours of *Blue Planet II* to watch on Netflix. This natural history of the oceans narrated by David Attenborough could hold my father's attention in a way narrative film could not. Together we watched the mesmerizing sway of underwater kelp forests and seagrass. We lost ourselves in the hypnotic drama of orca in the fjords of northern Norway herding shoals of herring into tighter and tighter balls to trap the prey near the water's surface. We felt the passive, narcotic calm of a flickering television.

Our eyes were riveted to a maze of coral, to Dumbo octopus and

Humboldt squid pulsing in the darkness. These other worlds, the distant diversity of the ocean's benthic depths, becalmed us.

There were no experts in our television room. No marine biologists or oceanographers. We were all on equal, mystified footing, encountering unknown creatures we had never before contemplated, plunging ourselves into the scale of a planet that made the scale of the personal feel, well, tiny. The ocean is an enchanted and impossible world. We learned it contains 90 percent of the planet's biomass.

In the final episode of *Blue Planet II*, we were confronted with an awful scenario: the ocean's enchanted and impossible world becoming a warmed-up, bleached, acidified, plastic-poisoned grave.

The lesson of oceans is that the tiny affects the vast. There is no far-off distant. We are all inside the scale whether we choose to see it or not.

Together, my sons and I were learning: to see with greater clarity the deep lives that rumble below the radar, to hear the grounding music of the non-speaking world.

What surprised us is that even in the midst of urgency and emergency, there could be calm. There could be flat days when the water smoothed every disturbance into a glassy plane. There could be stormless days when the water became a serene mirror. My father was sick, he was well. Just like the planet. He was dying, he was living. We existed without a solid shore, in the great sea of the moment. Attritional. Incremental. Set somewhere between two points. No clear plot or path.

Chronic illness, like climate change, I came to see, toppled the idea of getting to the other side.

One evening, I realized we were acquiring the posture of a family huddled on a lifeboat. The stress of living among overlapping spheres of illness and wellness was turning us small and inward.

I thought about the tiny vessel that had become our world as I worked the wooden oars, moving around and around in circles. Was the dream to stay in the lifeboat where we sat, with the stormy waters rocking us, our faces tilted skyward, praying for a sunbeam?

I saw how caregiving could contract a world to the size of a house or a bed; fasten you to the caregivee: the one, very particular person you were trying to keep alive.

Filial caregiving had lent a form to my life, delineated my purpose, responsibilities, what I was meant to do. I saw how much less graspable it was to care for countless fragile ecosystems, how much more challenging to block the construction of a pipeline, to invent new arts for living on a damaged planet, to forge new multispecies collectivities.

The lifeboat is a bloated signifier in climate discourse. It is a harbinger of our collective fate if the great ship of humanity fails to change course. The lifeboat is also, in the present tense, what we see drifting in the Mediterranean—a reminder of global governmental failures and the ascendance of neoliberalism where too frequently care and worth are delimited or "incentivized" by market value.

These days whole countries are being described as lifeboats. A lifeboat region is defined as an area that will remain habitable in the event of catastrophic climate change. Ireland and England, we are told, will be the last remaining refuges as displaced and stressed populations flee sea level rise and wildly destructive weather, as suffering disperses. Suffolk, Bedfordshire, Wales, and the Western Highlands— all possible safe havens in the event of disastrous flooding.

The International Organization for Migration estimates between twenty-five million and one billion additional refugees will be created by man-made climate change by 2050. Where will they go?

Who will rescue them from the waves?

The lifeboat narrative depends on a fallacious premise: that there is a dearth of lifeboat space and a shortage of provisions in the world. This kind of sink-or-swim scarcity thinking perpetuates the distributive injustices that have allowed "sacrifice zones" to emerge. It denies resources to those who have lost the most. It impoverishes the commons by presenting human nature as inevitably governed by fear, self-interest, and violent individualism.

To lift care out of the lifeboat is to reveal the not-so-subtle violence behind the idea of limited caring capacity.

If the "lifeboat scenario" is connected to the genocidal breakdown of compassion and mutual aid, a second "collective scenario" offers the promise of other ethical, political, and behavioural ways forward. In the latter story, we are capable of building and maintaining a public disaster-response infrastructure that exists to help everyone, i.e., a radical "survivalism." No one, no thing, is expendable.

A few facts about lifeboats: A lifeboat is a safe haven until it meets a bigger storm. A lifeboat is a safe haven until more people want to get on board. A lifeboat is, in essence and by definition, provisional. It requires a vital adjustment of your body and its needs. It may get you through the emergency but it cannot carry you forever.

What happens after the dream of drifting away from danger, after the safe moment in clear, beautiful water?

For months I cultivated the focus necessary to care for my father and continue working, but as I travelled deeper into my father's illness, care required breaking away from the family cave, countering protectionist tendencies and the fantasy of arrogant independence. We needed help.

We spent hours in clamorous waiting rooms and memory clinics, in hospital wards full of beeping monitors. Despite the privacy curtains, the hush of communal living and collective being suddenly loudened. In crisis, partitions become thin as cloth.

This chorus, with its tune of fragility and finitude, instructed me. This choral song of ill bodies and aging bodies, bodies reliant on civic and medical infrastructure, on public care and support, alerted me to what I wasn't hearing—the pull and flow of dialysis, the ocean roar of ultrasound, the overheated precarity and messy faltering beneath the smooth flow of everyday life.

In the waiting room, I saw that care is not always tied to salvage and repair. The hospital was a storm ward. Poor, sick, disfigured, alone. Social vulnerability was made plain.

Then Hurricane Harvey was in the news (then Irma, then Maria), and I saw the disastrous degree to which weather emergencies deepened other, prior vulnerabilities. All those people fighting to find a way to shore, whose world was now more water than earth, more wavering than solid. I wondered: Where did they get their meds when the pharmacies closed, when floodwaters ruined essential drugs? Did collective viral loads increase?

Before Houston residents could lose hope after Hurricane Harvey, a flotilla arrived. Volunteers from across Texas, and from neighbouring states such as Louisiana, poured into the city on boats to join the official rescue effort. In late summer of 2017, as rain pummelled down and roads rushed like rivers, emergent modes of assembling and collectivity were unfolding.

The fleet of boats in Houston recalled, for me, a scene several months before when a group of Pacific Islanders paddled halfway across the world to visit the Canadian tar sands. Prime Minister Trudeau's recently approved pipelines will unleash catastrophic climate change—for Pacific Islanders this means rising sea levels threatening their homes, communities, and cultures. So, in May 2017, the Pacific Climate Warriors embarked on a journey to bear witness to the project responsible for unleashing destruction on their homelands. Along the way, they built solidarity with Indigenous communities in Canada whose traditional territories are threatened by the tar sands.

The Pacific Climate Warriors showed that care could have a wide circumference. Around the time the Pacific Climate Warriors were in Northern Alberta touring the tar sands region with local First Nations, I was asked to do a magazine interview discussing my creative and scholarly work. I told the interviewer that the time I spent taking care of my father was helping with my research on climate change. It's deepening the work, I said, because it's making me understand durational care. It's allowing me to move out of the time of crisis into the time of the chronic. It has forced me to attend to alternative forms of time—to notice the slow, constant, and non-acute as something worthy of response and care.

Thank you, universe, she said.

What I was also trying to say, whether or not it came across, was that at our family's most vulnerable moments, I felt a breaking down of the opposition between caring for "one's own" and caring for the world.

*In memory of my father, Michael Maclear (1929-2018)*

**Note:**

The title of this essay leans on Rebecca Solnit's "Love and Lifeboats," in *A Paradise Built in Hell: The Extraordinary Communities That Arise in Disaster* (New York: Penguin, 2010).

# What Worries Us

# Wildfire

## ALISON COLWELL

---

### Monday, July 24, 2006

I flick on the radio while making breakfast. The familiar voices of CBC *Early Edition* fill the kitchen and I freeze, kettle midway to the sink. Our island is burning.

"A state of emergency was declared late Sunday night. One hundred and twenty residents have been evacuated...."

That's one-tenth of our population. Everything looks normal when I glance out the window. I set the kettle down, pour a dish of Goldfish crackers to distract the twins, and open my computer. Sleep deprivation and two-year-old twins have kept me ignorant: the fire is the only news on Facebook this morning. The fire started late yesterday and high winds overnight have doubled its size. It's burning in the new community park at the end of Georgia View Road, a property that reaches right over Galiano Island's spinal ridge. If the fire reaches the main road, the north-end residents will be trapped with no way to reach the ferry terminal. Checking Facebook. People need cat carriers, places to sleep. The Lionettes are making platters of sandwiches for the local firefighters who worked all night. Volunteers needed. Two little girls slept on pink velvet couches in Grand Central Cafe, waiting for morning and a ferry off the island.

On the floor behind me, Laura and Malcolm are fussing, hungry, and I reluctantly close the computer to make breakfast.

Like many residents, I came to Galiano to escape the craziness of Vancouver. Come for a week, a month, and never leave. The island heals people. Old wounds get buried in the routine of a small community, acceptance in a place where everyone knows who you are.

Evacuations, emergencies...they don't belong here.

———

The twins are strapped in their double stroller. It's nap time and the stroller is the only way to get them to sleep. I'm pushing them up the road, past the full parking lot outside Grand Central. I turn right. The traffic is stopped. It's not local traffic, but tourists waiting for a boat off the island. They're quiet, not like last week's bustling summer crowds. These people just want off a sinking ship.

We're not going to burn, I tell myself. I know all the local fire-fighters: Ron, Mike, Rolyn, Sean, and the others are out there right now, protecting the island, their own homes and families. And more firefighters are coming from Salt Spring, Victoria, and Vancouver. Overhead, the roar of a big water bomber blots out other sounds as it returns to the fire again and again with its belly full of water.

The noise of the planes and helicopters is keeping the twins awake. White flakes stand out against the dark blue stroller hood. Ash. Ash is falling. I pull the hood as far forward over them as I can and rush home. Abandoning the nap, I read them *Goodnight Moon* over and over again while listening to the weather forecast on the radio. More high winds are expected overnight.

*Is staying a mistake? Should I flee, too?*

## Tuesday, July 25, 2006

The twins haven't noticed the orange sky. Malcolm wants me to play in the sandbox with him, and Laura wants me to push her on the swing. But I can't play. I keep pausing, glancing up. The fire is five kilometres north of us. The winds are blowing toward us. I can feel smoke in my lungs, tightness when I breathe.

There are a hundred firefighters between the blaze and us. I should feel safe, but I don't.

"The Galiano wildfire is 90 percent contained," the CBC announcer drones from the portable radio on the patio table. "The fire remains at sixty-one hectares."

But if the winds flare up, if the fire heads south, I can't just pack the kids in the car and drive away. What if the last ferry of the day has already left?

Forecast is for high winds again.

*Why am I still here?*

## Wednesday, July 26, 2006

The evacuation notice has been lifted.

"Unless the winds shift..." say the news reports. The fire isn't out, but it's contained. BC Ferries is allowing tourists back onto the island. The winds died, and the firefighters held the line. One hundred and fifty acres have burned, but no houses. The water bomber has moved on. Firefighters are still working on the ground, but the crisis is over.

This time.

## Tuesday, May 27, 2008

My friend Christine meets me at the Georgia View park entrance. We park in the turnaround, unload kids and dog, our backpacks filled with water bottles and wet wipes and all the snacks three four-year-old kids could need. The first part of the trail is steep as it follows the overgrown logging road. The shallow ditch that borders the trail is thick with horsetails and ferns.

At the first junction we turn left, and the trail levels out. The kids call this Burnt Log Trail. The smell of fire is gone but charred stumps reveal the size of the blaze. Posted signs warn foragers not to pick mushrooms. The chemicals used to fight the fire have leached into the soil.

At the first turn, I look up the hillside, where small alder trees—still no taller than me—are springing up. The acres of slope are covered with long stems of foxgloves in every shade: white, pink, and deepest purple. No manicured garden has ever looked so excessive. Beautiful and invasive, they've colonized the fire zone. The kids pick individual blossoms to slide onto their fingers, soft gloves of purple, before they race to the largest fallen log where they can sit and eat their picnic. Beyond, a small stream burbles down the slope. Sparrows and robins call from the brambles. It feels like the land is beginning to heal, and my own memories of helplessness are also fading.

## Wednesday, March 14, 2018

The dawn light is grey when I arrive at the parking lot after dropping the kids off at the school boat. Rogan heels beside me as I hike up the trail into the Community Forest. The alder trees are still bare, rust-coloured catkins clinging to thin branches. The ditch is lined with swordferns and this year's new nettle plants. Seeing them reminds me I need to start harvesting for the upcoming nettle potluck. Prickly stems of wild rose push from the bank above, shadowed by the dark trunks of the firs beyond.

Then I reach the first junction. The edge of the old burn. Twelve years later and occasional blackened stumps are all that's left to show this was once the site of the Gulf Islands' largest forest fire in recorded history. Invasive Scotch broom threatens to overwhelm the new trails. Community work parties are held annually to try to keep down the broom. Unchecked, broom can reach eight feet tall, with stems thicker than my arm, choking the trails with impenetrable brush. Broom has swallowed the log where once I picnicked with the kids. One of the trails we worked so hard to clear last year is already impassable. Broom has consumed the hillside, crowding out native salal, trailing raspberry, and huckleberry.

My pants are wet with dew by the time I reach the top, the place where the trail curves back, following the top edge of the burn. Foxgloves are rarer now, coming up only at the edges of the trail. Robins cheep in alarm as Rogan and I pass. Commuter planes roar overhead, heading to Vancouver, just visible in the distance from the top of the ridge. A line of swans passes. A sooty grouse calls, its low thrum a reassuring heartbeat of the forest.

The scars are slowly healing. Burnt snags are slowly falling, their papery trunks holed by woodpeckers. Broom has pushed out the foxgloves and the blackberry, but eventually forest will reclaim the slope and the view will disappear. In the meantime, the creatures that live here have adapted to the changed landscape; deer stay on the fringes of the burn, and turkey vultures catch the thermals above.

If you hadn't lived through the fire, you might not recognize the trauma to the land or the signs of slow recovery; you might only appreciate the sense of open space. The fire changed the landscape, but it wasn't the "end times" I'd expected.

Summers seem drier now, and they seem to last longer than when I first came to this small island twenty-five years ago. Cedars are reddening, dying from lack of rain, and some of the grand firs too. But watching the changing landscape of the burn has taught me that nature continues to adapt, to change, and we, as a community, can play our role too. We can strive to build resilience in our environment, in our communities, and in the relations between the two. I believe this. And sometimes I can forget about the fire. Until summer comes, and I watch the moss curling back from the bedrock and I start to keep track of the days without rain.

There were ninety-two last summer.

# Hidden Gardens

**REED OSLER**

---

i. *Whatever impacts the ocean, or anything*
*living in the ocean, will impact us*

Some things are hidden
tucked away from view
secreted away in dark places
just beyond reach

Sometimes you catch a glimpse
the tide goes out
leaves moist rocks
covered in ragged weed
children flip them over and exclaim

A fish, flat face, bulging eyes
large fins, brown, mottled skin
looking back at them
mouth gulping, wide, open
and glistening eggs, the size of large pearls
round, yellow, laid neatly in rows

Everyone's eyes are opened
they want to know what it is

I take a look
dredge up memory
from the depths
a plainfish midshipman
dressed in a captain's uniform
bright buttons line its belly
light up the sea
A bottom dweller
come to the surface
to deposit its golden eggs

I have lifted thousands of rocks on beaches
hunched over, looking closely, waiting
for secrets to reveal themselves
I have never seen this

Rock after rock offers up
these spawning creatures
sometimes more than one
nestled in the muck
kids carefully replacing rocks
tucking the fish into their nests

Their large mouths hum
speak salty sea language
the creatures it conceals
in its fluid folds

What else do we fail to notice?
What vanishes before we get a chance
or take the time to see
a shimmer from another world


## ii. *Glass sponges filter the Howe Sound in one year—the entire body of water*

A world where
hands can't go
eyes can't see
lungs can't breathe

A world full of ancient animals
masquerading as plants
animals
towering above the sea floor
glass condominiums
eight storeys high
feasting on bacteria
in a sea so vast
they remain unseen

Skeletal silica structures
silently building reefs
on a barren sea floor
sheltering finned ones
shelled ones
many leggeds
swimming in and out
of glass fingers
once thought to be extinct
rediscovered not long ago

Where only submarines can reach
they gather in dark depths
blown into different shapes
cloud glass sponges
tubular glowing columns
finger goblets
ethereal otherworldly forms
anchored to rocks or other sponges
spreading into cities

Beneath turbulent waves
They pull in salty brine
pump it out again
in and out for millennia
cleaning these waters

Waters that generations
fed from and journeyed on
invisible threads tracing back in time
and out into the future
beyond vision
offering silent thanks for abundance
to ones they could not see
small creatures
houses of glass
filtering the sea

Now the surface reaches down
touches the deep
glass gardens
still invisible to many
not shielded from these
warmer more acidic waters
that slow their pumping down

A ripple from the depths reaches out
asking us to look beneath
asking us to see

## Note:

Italicized section titles are by Angela Stevenson, quoted in Abi Hayward and
    Brenden Dixon, "Glass Sponges, Climate Change and BC's Ocean Environment,"
    *The Tyee*, May 8, 2018, https://thetyee.ca/News/2018/05/08/Glass-Sponges
    -Climate-Change-BC-Ocean-Environment/.

# The Ends of the World

**RICHARD PICKARD**

---

## i. Thanksgiving in Victoria, October 2008

The lights went out just before 6:00 p.m., right after we'd sat down to turkey, stuffing, sweet potato mash, cranberry, and all the rest.

"Perfect timing," my father-in-law said.

"The blessing's already been said and received," said my mother-in-law.

The Brussels sprouts died on my tongue, but I stayed quiet, because I didn't want to worry the rest of the family. The thing was, I'd been reading enough about the social collapse that would follow climate change to know, in my heart, that this was the end.

And so we ate, and talked, and laughed, sharing stories and reflecting together on all sorts of small but important moments that, ten years on now, are mostly long forgotten.

Nearing forty, back then, I wasn't exactly surprised when the power came back, when it turned out not to have been the end after all.

Still, I knew that there'd come a day when the power wouldn't come back, and that it would indeed be the end.

That climate change would be real enough, soon enough, that we wouldn't be able to continue the feast.

## ii. North Coast Trail, July 2012

The previous summer had seen an earthquake in Japan that led to the Fukushima Daiichi nuclear crisis. Fever-dream animated maps had immediately begun showing rogue radiation sweeping across the North Pacific toward North America and Vancouver Island, bearing with it all sorts of detritus grabbed from Japan by the post-quake tsunami.

Long before the earthquake, a few of us in our men's monthly book club, Beer and Books, had already been talking about a multi-day hike. We chose the North Coast Trail—around the northern tip of Vancouver Island—when our most experienced member refused to hike the West Coast Trail for what would have been his twenty-third time. He allowed that he'd always wondered about the North Coast.

Once the quake hit Japan, our planning conversations kept drifting toward what signs of the disaster might show up on the North Coast Trail. As we motored from Port Hardy by boat to the drop-off point, however, looking ahead at six days and seventy-five kilometres of hiking, the notion of disaster became less and less notional.

The black bear grazing at the tide line, two hundred metres away from where we were put ashore, didn't help.

"Oh, he's always there," said the guide, predictably laconic.

"How was it?" we hazarded to the begrimed, haggard group whose hike was just ending where ours was beginning.

Pause.

One man spoke up. "It'll change you." That was all he said.

Long before this point, our group of readerly hikers had been cut to merely a pair of us, and things didn't look good. The only experienced potential hiker, the one who'd pushed us off the West Coast Trail, had bailed because he felt he wasn't physically fit enough for the North Coast. The spidery writer I was travelling with—at six feet two, fully six inches taller than me, but no heavier—could swim for miles and cycle for hours, but this didn't make him any less spidery, and we weren't scheduled to swim or cycle. It's possible that I was stronger, given what could generously be described as my lower centre of gravity, but this seemed irrelevant. After all, I'd never done an overnight hike in my life, my leather Tyrol hiking boots were twenty-eight years old, and, to keep our packs light, we'd decided against bringing either a satellite phone or bear spray. Also to keep the packs light, we'd brought only high-proof alcohol.

Two hours into that first morning, both my thighs cramped so hard on a ladder that I could go neither up nor down, until I found a way to climb without bending my knees. The second day, we took twelve hours to cover thirteen kilometres, often across loose rocks the size of human skulls, with the occasional near-vertical scramble and descent we could manage only by clinging to weathered ropes we never truly trusted. By day three, we had traded away one of our maps to four guys from Calgary, in exchange for part of the remarkable volume of alcohol they were still somehow carrying. As we neared Cape Scott Provincial Park on day five, we found someone from BC Parks blasting away with a gas-powered weed trimmer along a bog boardwalk; we were advised that just up the trail, she'd missed a spot roughly forty-five kilometres long.

But what of the earthquake and its aftermath?

Across the six days, we saw barely anything we could pin on the tsunami. Eventually a skiff turned up in California, a soccer ball in Alaska, a street sign in Hawaii, and a Harley-Davidson on Haida Gwaii (inside a storage container). Oceanographer and biogeochemist Jay Cullen and his Fukushima InFORM project were confident that the radiation would barely register, given the mass of the ocean, and their monitoring suggests that only 1/300 of the radiation found in BC salmon can be attributed to Fukushima. According to Cullen's team, the amount of Fukushima radiation consumed by an average salmon-eating West Coast human is about 1/30,000 of the annual dose an average Canadian normally receives from naturally occurring sources.

Our gruelling playtime on the North Coast Trail, which is a remarkable and beautiful stretch of sand and sea and forest, had occurred mostly in the traditional lands of the Tlatlasikwala. We had crossed the Nahwitti River, with its rich offshore fishing grounds that the Tlatlasikwala and other nations had relied on for millennia, and we'd never been more than a few kilometres from logging activity occurring within the last thirty years.

They're fantasies, these ideas of the "end of the world" or the "edge of the world."

Which doesn't mean that my left knee will ever work quite properly again, or that Fukushima will be inhabitable for humans again any time soon, or that capitalist/industrial humanity isn't in fact making the planet uninhabitable.

## iii. Glittering Wood Moss

Throughout the BC Southern Interior, in quiet small valleys where one or more settler waves gave up their ungrounded dreams of new ground, only to be succeeded by concreted towns and cities and highways blocking off larger valleys nearby, glittering wood moss plays a special role in illuminating the material form and extent of settler failure.

As elsewhere, cabins, sheds, and food and equipment caches for European settlement in the Thompson-Okanagan region came from cutting down trees and then piling them into structures intended to be permanent, or at least to gesture toward permanency. Log buildings, though, are by nature drafty contraptions, permeable to windblown dust or snow, to rainwater and snowmelt and insects. To caulk these gaps, settlers tried every local material they could think of, from mud to grass to strips of wood to cedar bark. As insulation and as binder for clay, glittering wood moss was regularly stuffed into these gaps, just as it was stuffed into pillows and mattress ticks, strewn as carpeting, bound over wounds, and possibly used (like sphagnum mosses) during menstruation.

In each clearing where you find such buildings' remains now, you will find mosses and other plants—glittering wood moss, *Hylocomium splendens*, often dominant among them—inexorably reclaiming the buildings, their materials, and the spaces where (from a plant community's perspective) they'd so briefly stood.

This unassuming but pervasive and long-standing species was helpful for so many generations of First Nations in what's currently known as Canada and for early peoples elsewhere across Russia, northern Europe, Scotland, and Sweden. Later, glittering wood moss was just as helpful for settlers in their spreading across Canada. In recent decades, this moss has been busily erasing the evidence here of failed settler activities—and yet it may not make it to the next time the world ends. In 2003, Swedish researchers found that by altering precipitation patterns, nitrogen levels, and temperature, climate change will almost certainly make things harder everywhere for glittering wood moss.

This species that was here for us so intimately, for so many settler and Indigenous beginnings, may be gone before the next great end.

Of course the world is always ending, just like it is always beginning. Usually, though, the demarcations between beginnings and endings are soft enough that we can pretend the world's just continuing merrily along: wine and weed trimmers in the wilderness, cheerful non sequiturs both.

I haven't forgotten how immediately the taste of Brussels sprouts died on my tongue.

Climate change will be just like that.

## Note:

To learn about the Integrated Fukushima Ocean Radionuclide Monitoring or INFORM network, please visit https://fukushimainform.ca/.

# The Prodigious

**EMILY McGIFFIN**

---

## i.

What can it hold for us, the future? I fear it
will betray us, as it has done in the past. Bhopal,
for instance, Fukushima, the lifeless basin that was once
the Aral Sea, those broken landscapes like foregone
conclusions. But as the pale sky grows thick with doubt
and as the river slides past, cold and boiling slick
around the crusting ice in this last trickle of declining
light, as the falling snow begins to whisper and nocturnal
creatures tiptoe in to claim the dusky fields, as the stifled
moonbeams, mountain ranges, birches standing patient,
all those shifting and unfathomable beings speak with singular
precision from their homes within the reeling solar system,
snow's veil swathes the ground like a collective silent wish.
I sit alone with a radio and the kettle's rising whistle, thinking
of the weather and the inland seas, the distant populations
held hostage by history's accruals, cruel politics, economics
of our imagined needs. In the snowy twilight, burdened
with the season and its losses, this cold might be predictable,

but never certain, and from the radio a live jazz concert unfurls,
sax, piano, drums and bass, the tune lively and familiar
though its name escapes me, I Should Care or Things Ain't
What They Used to Be, the new arrangement drawing
freshness from a tired standard. Outside, the mountain settles
somewhere in the clouds, the old moon lost amid the drifts
while pools of sulphur light fall on the mounded snow. Rising
through a distant concert hall, a gift of music. It is winter,
the notes unfold, they build and gather, but at any time
the sound could fall away, the theme dissolve, the pianist
could stand and bow, step off the stage and stride alone
into the swirling flakes, notes trailing from his hands
like glaciers ebbing up a mountainside, swallows falling
dead into a cornfield, and left behind the band might
fumble an apology while the audience sits gazing, baffled,
at silence and an empty stage, everyone alert now, waiting.

ii.

And as I wait, the animals begin to fill my dreams,
stepping from the shadows to accompany my sleep,
tiny golden frogs and hefty snails, antelopes, vast
swirling flocks of birds. They watch with quiet eyes
as I step into their realm. And as I walk, their green
recedes. It wilts to brown. Brown ripples from each step,
the grasses wither to bare soil, leaves shrivel on the trees.
A snail, sliding barefoot on the soil, drags a clod of dust
and probes, puzzled, at the heat with globule eyes,
searching for some patch of damp to lay its eggs.
Even as it glides the plants retreat. This, I see at last,
is disappearance. Our world transfigured as we watch.

Overcome, I sit down in the dust, on the cracked ground
beneath a wiry acacia and lean against its trunk.
A giraffe, shabby, thin, nosing at the leafless thornbush,
steps closer until it stands within a tree length of me.
It stands unmoving, watching me, ears flicking off the flies.
And then it folds its legs and lays its body on the hot
and stony earth. It blinks and snorts. Then, ponderously,
it lowers its head. Slowly, slowly, the elegant neck descends,
until its beautiful head lies there, gently, on my lap.
The nostrils flare and I smell the blast of animal breath.
It moves its slender jaw and the hairs on its chin prickle
against my legs and its head lies heavy, resting.
It blinks its long-lashed eyes. They slowly close. It sighs.
And when I lift my hand to touch its ears, its tufted
ossicones, to stroke its cowlicked forehead and the mottled
hair along its throat, I feel beneath my hand its slowing breath,
its own dreaming, its return to the savannah of its ancestors.
We ask one another, how did we become so lonely?
We have each been here, side by side. How can we bear
such estrangement? I lay my hands on the giraffe as it sleeps
and wake to a city park, a line of maples, an expanse
of ungrazed lawn trodden only by people and their dogs.
And the absent animals arrive in the night, calling.
What must I do to return the blessing of their visits? I must
remember them. I must listen. And somehow do as they ask.

# What the Sea Eats

**COLLEEN DOTY**

We moved to Galiano Island because Mom didn't like the city. She'd shake her head as if to rid herself of the memory: "You can't have five bloody chickens in that place."

In Vancouver, neighbours complained about the straw bales she put in boulevards to grow potatoes. "People like to forget where their food comes from," Mom said.

During our daily walk, she'd yell, litter tongs in hand, at whoever tossed cigarette butts into the street. "Those butts end up in the ocean! What kind of future are my kids going to have if people like you kill the fish?" The litterers would take a look at her, me at her side, and baby Grant on her back. "Sorry," they would usually say, then crouch down to pick up their butts.

We used our dining room window as a lookout. A car would slow and stop at the curb. Mom would look up from feeding Grant in his high chair. "Megan, get your shoes on," she'd say to me. "I have a feeling about this one. They're eating fast food." Sure enough, within seconds, we'd see a car door open and a bag of garbage tossed into the street. "Let's go!" Mom would have already unclicked Grant and be running outside with him in her arms, me not too far behind. She'd knock on the driver's side until they rolled down their window. "Hey, how would you like it if I dumped garbage in front of your home?"

Daddy told her she should be careful.

She told him she could handle things herself, thank you very much.

Daddy said our move to a tiny island of a thousand people was his leap of faith. I wasn't sure what that meant, exactly. It had something to do with him quitting his job at the university, and us leaving all our friends in Vancouver. I really missed my best friend, Stacy, who lived down the block from us. We had known each other since we were babies. I would be making new friends when kindergarten started in the fall, Mom said.

Grant was too little to care about leaving Vancouver. After a couple of weeks in our new home in the forest, Grant couldn't remember anything about the house where he was born.

Lucky him.

---

Since we moved here, every day is a beach day, and today it's Mom's turn to take us.

"Bellhouse Beach," Mom says to Daddy as she gathers water bottle and hats.

"Have fun," Daddy says, fixing another leak under the sink, his body sticking out from the cabinets.

I've been to Bellhouse Beach once before, and we love it. The beach is wide, the sand is silky smooth, and the last time we came, we saw whales swim by in the distance. The walk there is also fun. Daddy built a platform for me on the back of the stroller so I can stand between the handlebars while Grant rides inside. We walk past blackberry bushes, rickety wooden fences, and farms with cows that stare back at us like we're pictures on a wall.

Off the gravel road there is a narrow path, lined by rosehips and old pear trees. This is the path we take down to the beach. When we look up, our sky is dotted with pears that hang like coloured clouds: some are yellow, some bright green, and others have streaks of red on them.

"In a month or so we can shake these trees and it will rain pears!" Mom says.

"Yay!" Grant squeals.

At the end of the path a bench overlooks the flat beach. The smell of salt water and seaweed fills my nose.

"Tide's out," Mom says. We park the stroller, and Grant and I run down the giant rock steps, over the rippled sand, to the water's edge.

Grant stamps his feet into the shallow water. I search for a shell, just the right one, not broken, maybe with a creature inside. I look back to the beach. Mom carries our stuff and finds a place to lay out a towel. I run back to her. She smiles when I show her the hinged pink and purple clam in my hand.

I start to make a sandcastle with a moat. Mom is in her quiet zone. I can tell, even with her sunglasses on, her eyes watch Grant. She tracks the ocean in the distance. I find a salal leaf on the sand and press it into the side of the castle.

"If you are ever on a beach somewhere, on open ocean, and you see water all pulling back at once, run to higher ground. That means a tsunami is coming."

I stop what I'm doing. *Tsunami*. I'd heard that word before. Mom and Dad had talked about the time a tsunami washed away a town they were visiting, far away.

"A tsunami could be taller than our house," Mom says. "After the Indian Ocean earthquake, so many little girls like you died. More girls than boys. They didn't know how to swim or climb trees. Many girls were at home looking after younger siblings when the waves came. This beach reminds me of those beaches in Thailand."

My hands are cold. I feel sick. Scared of dying, of losing Mom and Dad. Down the beach Grant throws shells into the water. He's having fun. I wish I could be like him.

"Could a tsunami happen here?" I ask.

"On this island, unlikely," Mom says. "The Indian Ocean tsunami was caused by the earth's plates moving against each other. Another cause of earthquakes comes from the ocean floor destabilizing with climate change. The Northern Hemisphere, in particular, will experience more earthquakes as glaciers rapidly melt and severe storms deposit layers of debris onto the ocean floor. More earthquakes mean more tsunamis in our part of the world."

I think about what Mom has told me. She used the word *unlikely*. There are so many problems with the earth because of what humans have done to it. Air heating up, ocean floor like Jell-O, water that could drown me.

But I can run fast and I know how to climb.

Grant laughs and lifts up a jellyfish. He shows us the dripping, clear goo. Mom smiles back at him. "That kid," she says to me.

I nod. That kid won't hold me back.

---

Daddy's day to take us to the beach. Bellhouse Beach again. Daddy parks the stroller at the end of the trail. I jump off the platform and Grant climbs out, toy dump truck in hand. He kicks off his Crocs, but I decide to keep my sandals on so I can explore rocks and barnacles.

We run down to the beach.

"Tide's coming in," Daddy says. "We have at least an hour before the water comes right up to the wall."

The sea seems bumpy today. Mom told me to never turn my back to it.

We skip rocks. Daddy's the best. Nine jumps, his record for today.

Grant's throws are so funny. They go in every direction. He gives up and loads his dump truck with sand.

The rumbling starts before we see anything. From the sand my feet vibrate. Noise rattles my brain. It's coming from everywhere: the sky, the ground, the sea. Daddy and I look at each other.

"Here come the ferries," he says. A loud horn blows. A small ferry comes around the corner. People on deck wave at us. Grant empties his dump truck.

A much larger ferry follows right behind the smaller one.

Then, the sea slides away like a blanket off a bed. Grant's dump truck is suddenly sucked out. He screams. Daddy looks worried, like he often does when Grant cries.

But this time the worry feels different to me.

Grant runs after his truck as waves carry it out. I see what's going to happen. Grant doesn't know the waves are going to come back in. And they're going to come back huge.

"I'm coming, Grant!" Daddy runs to get him.

My stomach drops. Grant's getting rescued.

I know what I have to do.

While Daddy runs to get Grant, I race in the opposite direction toward the steps up to the trail. At the bottom of the steps I quickly turn. Daddy has scooped Grant under one arm. Waves bigger than me follow them up the beach.

Run! Up the stone steps. One foot after the other. At the top, I look back down to the beach. Daddy doesn't see me. His eyes are focused on the sand in front of him as he runs away from the water.

I don't stay to watch what happens next.

The forest path will take me out to the road.

---

I am on my own. I've been running a long time. Ravens caw high in the trees. They've been following me along the road, leapfrogging in the canopy above. I try to block them out. Why aren't they flying away, escaping to the mountains?

In my head, Mom's voice, "Run to higher ground," pushes my numb legs up the hill toward home.

I will not be one of the girls who dies.

Almost there. I see our driveway in the distance and wonder how much time I have.

I hear a car from behind. It slows, then crawls, along beside me.

From the window a grey-haired lady leans out. "Are you allowed to be alone like this?" An older girl sits beside her in the front seat. I've seen them around the island.

I slow my running. I don't know how to answer. Usually I wouldn't be alone, but I'm doing what Mom told me to do. I look behind me down the hill, past farms and forest, in the direction of the ocean I can no longer see, where I left Daddy and Grant.

"A tsunami came." Tears drip on my shirt. I've stopped running. My whole body shakes.

The car stops.

"Tsunamis can't reach this island. Vancouver Island blocks them." The lady smiles and seems sure of herself. Was Mom wrong about tsunamis? What did I see?

"Come with us, Megan. We'll find your family." I freeze. She knows my name. She reaches behind her and opens the car door from the inside.

The big kid smiles.

I decide to climb in.

"Ferry waves can seem huge if the tide is right," the big girl says.

The lady turns her car around in the middle of the road and drives down the lane I had just run up.

From the car window I see the lower road is dry. The trees are standing. The fences are in place. Grass sways in the wind. The ocean has not come up. Ahead, where the beach trail meets the road, I see Daddy with some dog walkers, people talking, looking in different directions. Daddy has a faraway look. Grant, sucking his thumb, is in his arms. Daddy watches the car approach and then smiles big when he sees me in the back seat. I hear another grown-up whistle, then call down to the beach. "We found her!"

When the lady stops the car, Daddy opens the door and pulls me into a hug. Me in one arm, Grant in the other.

I can't stop crying.

**Notes:**

Bill McGuire, "Potential for a Hazardous Geospheric Response to Projected Future Climate Changes," *Philosophical Transactions of the Royal Society A* 368, no. 1919 (2010): 2317–45.

United Nations Development Programme, "Women and Children Are 14 Times More Likely Than Men to Die During a Disaster," *Gender and Disaster Risk Reduction*, Policy Brief, Office for the Coordination of Humanitarian Affairs (2013): 1–6.

# In Between Red, Blue, and Green

**DEBLEKHA GUIN**

As she emerged from her sleepy cocoon, she took in the sounds of the intensifying rain and inhaled a deep breath of damp air. When her feet met the sharp chill of the bare floor, she jolted awake.

> *damn*
> *fell asleep before stoking the fire or*
> *making today's to-do list*

A barrage of tasks swirled through her mind as she left her bedroom.

> *finish the Climate Matters report*
> *submit the Salish Harvest application*
> *email the team about not being able to give advances*
> *sort logistics for the visioning meeting*
> *review the water district bylaws*

She hovered briefly at the end of the hall as her brain rerouted from autopilot. Most mornings she'd move toward the kettle in the kitchen, but today she veered to the living room in hopes of reviving yesterday's fire.

*arrange child care*
*figure out why the hydro bill is going off the charts*
*make something for tonight's potluck*
*get cream for coffee*
*try to squeeze in some yoga*

She continued to recite her list as she knelt before the wood stove and cracked open the door. Lists generally helped to orient her: they anchored her day and gave it shape. But they had the opposite effect today. This morning's inventory prompted a low-level wave of panic, and a wry rebuke of her life choices.

*ah, the "freedom" of working from home*
*on a small gulf island*

Sorting through the paltry scraps at the bottom of the kindling basket, she coached herself against interpreting this lapse in her ability to sustain the temperature of her home as a sign of being out of sync with the changing seasons or the flow of the day that had scarcely begun. She was eager to take the more optimistic view.

*these meagre coals have promise*

She blew on them with all she had.

---

Perched beside the wood stove, coffee in hand, she felt the rush of the strong brew and basked in the heat emerging from the fire. As the chill abated, she relaxed enough to notice the condensation forming where the cool window met the warming sill, and admire the calming soft-focus effect it gave to the view beyond. Not quite ready to dive into work, she paused to genuinely take in what was outside.

*I have stared at, and past, this view for seventeen years*
*variations on the theme of green*
*not breathtaking by postcard standards*

*but I see lots thriving out there*
*when I bother to really look*
*the slope of shiny salal*
*feathery splashes of ocean spray*
*the stand of red currant poised to pop*
*soon to beckon a host of hummingbirds*

*the mix of firs and cedars young and old*

*oh*

*but there are those cedars over there*
*I can't believe how abruptly they've died*
*lush green only last year*
*their boughs now hanging*
*scruffy and brittle*

Her head fell to her chest and she let out an involuntary groan. Her mind tumbled down a despairing rabbit hole that made the mounting tensions of her task list embarrassingly insignificant. Pondering the view her daughter might inherit, the quality of her internal deliberation shifted. As if addressing a chorus of her peers, her thoughts coalesced into something more closely resembling an intimate climate report. No: a eulogy.

*a dark shade of red is creeping into the green expanse outside*
*my window*
*burnt orange might be more painfully apt*

*and despite the current deluge of rain*
    *it screams of thirst*

*this is the colour of the tree of life's gradual demise*

*mighty western redcedar are rendered feeble and desolate*
    *their roots disintegrating under the cyclical stress of*
        *summers too dry*
        *winters too wet*
    *their solid stance threatened by accelerating winds*

The fire in the stove was now in full force. Its crackle and roar interrupted her disheartening thoughts about the dying cedars and what their fate meant in the grand scheme. She tentatively damped down the flue, and returned to her reflection from a different vantage point.

    *but there is still so much vibrant green*

    *is it disingenuous to fade out what's thriving to emphasize*
        *what's in peril?*

    *it might be what's needed to wake us up, and turn the tide*
    *but what are the costs of such selective seeing?*

    *fixating on scarcity and loss*
        *the frail and finite*
    *can make us*
    *stingy with the present*
    *and each other*

Wrapping her hands more snugly round the curve of her beloved cup, she found herself lost in a typical summer scene: a cast of Galiano characters bathed in the golden hues of the sinking sun at Montague

Beach. Ceremonially, they gravitate to the driftwood pews settled along the shoreline to share a meal, revel in animated conversation, and then savour the quieting colours of the day's last light.

------------

Was the spontaneous summoning of this gathering an indication of the counterbalance she sought?

*in the long run*

> *aren't we better off*
> *cultivating a love of place and*
>     *each other?*
> *noticing and tending to*
> *sources of open-hearted wonder*
>     *instead of living at the mercy of*
>     *suffocating apprehension*

Her calves fell asleep as she crouched before the stove, compulsively jabbing at the burning logs.

*then again*

> *is failing to grasp the more worrisome long-view that persists*
> *behind the awe-inspiring close-ups of our local lives*
>     *not just another form of numbing out*
>
>     *of overlooking the forest for the trees?*

Standing up, she tried to shake out the pins and needles in her legs before moving to her desk to rifle through scattered files and paper piles. Assembling the documents she needed to get down to work kept her busy, but it didn't completely distract her from nagging curiosity about her own emotional evasiveness.

> *why do I so rarely let myself feel sorrow about the sorry state of*
> *things?*

> *when it comes right down to it*
> *I'm afraid that feeling the full*
> *weight of it all*
> *will obliterate my optimism and faith in humanity*
> *eradicate my capacity for spontaneous joy*
> *engulf me in inescapable grief*

Startled by the rawness of this insight, she stopped in her tracks and briefly softened her stance before taking a defiant gulp of coffee.

> *I can't function*
> *let alone raise a healthy and resilient child*
> *from such a bleak space*

> *I can't afford the indulgence of surrendering to*
> *the red of righteous rage or*
> *the paralysis of feeling blue*

Yanking the charger from the wall, she marched into the kitchen, cleared a space on the crowded table, and fired up her laptop before realizing this was no way to begin.

> *first a walk to clear my head*

---

Her face tingled as she stepped into the expanse of crisp air. As the sun rose above the ridge, she felt the moisture from the early morning rain begin to evaporate. Her feet sprang to life as she pulled back her sweatshirt hood and found a comfortable stride under the clearing sky. Taking in the smell of mist rising out of moss-covered earth, she marvelled at the morning sunshine as it shimmered through the glistening cedar boughs, and was lifted by the singsong chirping of birds, and the startling whoosh of a raven overhead.

# field notes from the wide zone

**INDRA SINGH**

Doubled over a pond, a creek, the ocean. Pore over these moments at the pace of extinction. I came up to the surface at the Great Barrier Reef. Oh let's drink in the sea oh let's scrub in the salt. Refreshed, I came up to the surface off the Florida Keys. Distance compresses into youth. I step into ocean temperatures degrees higher as these moments shimmer on my memory current. Measurements inform me of how to rethink these visits. Over and over. Inch for inch. Degree for degree. We're exhilarated by the speed, aren't we? It's coming so—fast.

# The Change

## LISA SZABO-JONES

"C'est la catastrophe!" He gestures at the sky, the sun, his arms flailing upward. This seventy-odd-year-old French man, a fellow pilgrim on this 850-kilometre Camino walk, talks too much. Alex is hopeful she will never see him again after this moment. For now, though, they (his wife included) share what meagre shade this tree offers. Alex follows the arc of his arms. Not a cloud in the sky. It is early June, mid-morning, and forty degrees Celsius and climbing. Sweat slips over his face. He daubs repeatedly: neck, forehead, mouth. Spittle gathers at the corners of his lips. His wife, as short and wiry as he, sits beside him. She smiles, nods often, but does not speak. He introduces himself and his wife: Bernard and Ginette. They occupy the only log under the tree. Alex sits among the tree's roots, which smell faintly of urine and oranges. She notes the power-bar wrappers that litter the tree's roots, some folded into small squares and wedged into the crevices like prayer notes. She glances at the couple, shifts her weight.

Overhead, five or six black shapes circle, ride the updraft. They're too high to identify. By their numbers and size, she guesses griffon vultures. Alex takes out her phone. There's still cell reception. The bird app offers little. She searches Wikipedia. To contain mad cow disease, she reads, the European Union banned farmers from leaving livestock carcasses in the fields. Vulture numbers declined and behaviour altered. Farmers claim this ban and a scarcity of wild carrion compelled vultures to prey on livestock—Alex's eyebrows rise—and, it appears, to feed on humans. She reads how a fifty-two-year-old woman, hiking in the Pyrenees, fell to her death. How it took rescuers forty-five minutes to reach her body—or what little remained: clothing, shoes, bones. How they saw vultures circling, but did not make the connection. Alex follows other links. She finds an animated re-enactment on YouTube; she mutes the sound. She catches a headline: "France is facing a nasty animal epidemic: starving vultures." She opens and skims a PDF. Scientists contend the transport of carcasses and the incineration plants increased carbon dioxide emissions. She learns Spain authorized feeding areas. Griffon populations rebounded and their range continues to grow. To farmers' outrage, griffons remain a protected species. Alex pinches her nose. What a mess of facts and exaggeration: mad cow disease to vultures to climate change to vigilante farmers. It seems a stretch. She types in "names for groups of vultures": a wake. She snorts; certainly, some revelation is at hand. She closes the browser, looks up. The couple eye her expectantly. Alex grins, points to the sky. "Quel oiseau magnifique!"

Bernard and Ginette gaze upward, then back at her. Alex flaps her T-shirt. Sweat traps in the folds of her belly, under her breasts, the crack of her ass, anywhere there is crevice or shelf. She blows down her top. Bernard wipes the back of his neck. "La menace est énorme! Non, ce n'est pas normal!" He shakes his head. A spatter of his sweat hits her. "C'est le réchauffement global!"

Her French is basic, enough to hear the obvious, to parrot back. "Oui, global."

"C'est la faute du capitalisme!"

"Oui, et les hommes."

Bernard rocks back, slaps his thighs, opens his arms wide. "Tout le monde est complice!"

She pulls herself up, hoists her alpine pack onto her back, straps on her hiking poles. She holds out her cellphone, asks if he will take her photo. She is too self-conscious to take selfies in front of people. She turns her back to the tree, smiles. She regards the photo: a puffy middle-aged face, blotchy and sweaty, stares back. She thanks him, waves, and plods on.

The path is steep, open switchback. Over the next four hours, Alex climbs, stops, climbs, stops, watches the steady flow of hikers pass her. The customary greeting *bon camino*, at first charming, now irritates her; she nods in response. She spots Bernard and Ginette, in their matching yellow T-shirts, following lower on the trail. Bernard gestures as he talks. Alex sighs. She had hoped the Camino would be solitary, with frequent stretches without people. She gauges the couple's progress, how long it will take them to reach her. She stops, sips water. The pasture lands spread across the valley and hillsides. Five vultures float below. Alex feels like a faucet; sweat pours. She takes shallow breaths to bring her heart closer to a resting rate. The skipped beats, though, create breathlessness, then vertigo, as the blood flow surges and her heartbeat returns. Her doctor assures her this is of little concern, just another undeniable sign of "the Change." She looks down at her belly, that persistent thickness around her waist. She thinks about her lunch to come: fresh sourdough, Ossau-Iraty, a local cheese made from Manech sheep's milk, Basque cake. She worries what the heat may do to the cheese. Alex starts at a clatter of rocks. The French couple make the bend below her, wave, and smile. She waves back, turns, continues to climb.

Alex swears, jabs the hiking poles into the ground, and pulls. She is not here for some mid-life spiritual awakening or penance. She walks the French Way because she needs to lose weight, an "a-tone-ment," she tells people who ask. They laugh, but she detects their glances, quick, up and down. They leave her with platitudes: "Don't think about it"; "This is natural"; "You have to adapt"; "It's just a cycle"; "Change your behaviour." Change her behaviour. She uses the cattle and sheep ruts as steps, leans into the high neck of her leather boots, pushes up. Two hours of this and a slight heat begins to irritate her left heel. She grimaces. Aerobics classes, cycling, swimming, the gym, Pilates, yoga, even fucking meditation. She tried the Mediterranean, ketogenic, paleolithic, vegetarian, vegan, mindful eating. She wipes the sweat away from her eyes. She eyes the sky. The sun is a blank gaze. The weather, her aging body: it changes everything.

After another hour of climbing the dirt path, she tastes diesel and a tinge of perfume and sulphur. She climbs over a rise, steps onto asphalt. She hears a grunt and whoosh; pebbles roll off the road's edge. She sees nothing. She drops her pack, drinks some water. The smell hits her. A metre away, a red fox, not long dead, its guts streaked along the pavement, reaches for the road's shoulder. A shadow travels across the pavement, cuts across the fox, circles back, larger, slower. Alex looks up, stiffens. The griffon, yellow eyes, black smudge along the cutting edge of its beak, glides toward, passes over her. She exhales, laughs, wanders to the cliff edge, rises on her toes, and stretches open her arms, amazed at the distance she has climbed. She lowers her arms, stills, closes her eyes. Anxiety sinks, curls into her stomach. The heat blooms and washes through her. Sweat soaks her, trickles into her ear. The anxiety slips away. She steps backward and trips. She lands hard, rolls into the road, swears at the pain. The hot pavement burns her cheek. She can see the blue sky, a contrail. A pebble skips behind her and there is a scrape like metal on rock. She sits up, freezes. A griffon perches on the road, near the fox. Alex reaches into her pocket, pulls out her phone, and takes a selfie. The heat rising from the asphalt prompts her to pocket her phone and keep walking.

Alex is euphoric, thrills at her earlier encounter with the vulture, how it didn't even budge when she stood up and continued on her way. She sits now in the shade of a small tree, airing her feet, preparing to eat. She wiggles her toes. "Madame Alex!" Bernard and Ginette approach. Despite the ascent and heat, they remain enthused. They join her in the shade and take out their lunch. She empties her plastic bag. Bernard leans in; Ginette, silent, sits slightly behind him. They openly inspect each item of her lunch. Bernard lingers on the sweaty cheese, says nothing about the flattened cake. Alex shifts, feels a wave of heat. Sweat beads her upper lip. She bites and tugs on the softened bread crust, uses two hands to grip and pull. She watches Ginette place a tea towel on the grass, set out a small knife, open a paper bag, unwrap a small, crusty country loaf, open a small container of chèvre. She offers Alex a fresh grape tomato. She declines. Bernard asks Alex if she knows about the tragedy: a woman and something about bones or bears. He speaks too fast for her to follow. Bones, bears, she shrugs, smiles, and nods at him, apes his outrage, throws her hands skyward. "Quelle horreur!"

She left Bernard and Ginette ages ago and has met no one else since. Her stomach rumbles again. She follows a narrow path higher into the mountains, into a thunderhead. She regrets attempting the full twenty-four kilometres in one day, wonders how much farther to the end. Alex shivers. Sudden weather turns happen in mountains, but this is ridiculous. The wind gusts bring rain squalls, fog, and a temperature drop. She winces. Thunder cracks, but thankfully, no lightning. Just in case, she puts the rubber tips back on her hiking poles. Rain hits her face. She leans forward as she walks, occasionally stumbles. When the fog finally lifts and the rain stops, the sun has settled low on the horizon. The wind persists. She stops, studies the surrounding crags. She does a double take. She sees a man in dark grey sitting on a boulder high above her. He shifts and she realizes the man is a vulture. It is enormous. She gasps. A bearded vulture? This would be a rare sighting. These birds, legend has it, snatch elderly women. She curses not bringing her binoculars. Bearded vultures, she recalls, prefer bone marrow. They wait until the other birds and scavengers pick the bones clean. Alex imagines the sight of the birds carrying the larger bones into the air, dropping them. She shivers again. She needs another layer. She walks to a rock shelf, drops her pack, unzips her Gore-Tex jacket, takes out and puts on her fleece jumper. She looks over the edge. Her stomach drops; a familiar anxiety builds. She quickly unzips her coat and fleece, guzzles water. Her gut spasms. The heat rolls through her, sweat streams down her sternum. She turns into the wind, her back to the edge. She waits for the sweat to dry before she zips back up, admires her collapsible HydraPak water bottle. She squeezes the walls. It flops limp. Pops up. Flops limp. The fog is returning. The vulture is gone. She feels a light spray of rain, turns her face upward, closes her eyes. As she moves to pack up, a sharp, tearing heat rips across her heel. She hisses. The rock is wet, but she sits anyway, removes her boots and socks. She stands and limps to her pack, to her first aid kit. Her stomach pitches.

Above the fog line, the sun is now a visible glow backlighting the mountains. Bernard and Ginette emerge from the fog, near the rock ledge. Ginette spots Alex's pack on the rock outcrop, its spilled contents, and points. Bernard walks over to the wet ledge, sees the familiar phone abandoned by the boots. He looks to Ginette. He scans the rocks, calls out, "Allô! Madame Alex!" Silence. He cups his mouth, shouts louder. Ginette turns, calls out. Bernard lowers onto his hands and knees, crawls to the edge, peers over. The fog obscures the ground. "Madame Alex!" Ginette joins Bernard, picks up Alex's phone. It is unlocked and opens onto images. She taps her husband. Bernard gasps at the photo. "Mais non! Ce n'est pas possible!" They look at one another. The photo captures a blue sky; Alex is smiling, and in the background, a vulture stares into the lens.

# Are We Facing the Death
# of the Tree of Life?

**SUZANNE FOURNIER**

Above my North Galiano garden, there are thirteen stately trees, so massive and comforting that I call them my beloved elephants. All but two are western redcedar, rightly known as the arborvitae or tree of life. I often pause on my way down to my valley garden to gaze at their massive trunks. I love the tall cathedral silence over which they preside. I soak in their welcoming essence, smelling the pungent feathery foliage and the striped bronze bark. I feel as if they recognize me and that those who pass by are cleansed by their healing branches. Beside the path, a branch collar on one cedar forms a "green man" face, so beloved and familiar to our son that he would not tolerate plans to cut trees to get more sunlight on our garden. The cedars, we all hope, are here to stay.

Cedar has long been honoured as the tree that sustained life on Canada's West Coast, offering up its wood to the Indigenous Coast Salish on Galiano, and other First Nations, for houses, planks, and canoes. Babies can be cradled in cedar-made carriers warmed with its aromatic fronds. Strips of inner cedar bark can be woven into warm wind- and water-resistant hats and capes; cedar baskets can carry clams or hold water.

For millennia, western redcedar, or *Thuja plicata*, has been a cultural keystone species, used in the most practical ways but also as a sacred and healing resource. Its branches are used to expunge interior and exterior spaces of negative influences. Pungent cedar oil has both antifungal and antibacterial properties and can help solve respiratory or reproductive problems. Branch tips and bark were once boiled to treat rampant tuberculosis in the post-European-contact era. Chewing cedar leaves relieves stomach pains, while external poultices and decoctions can help heal damaged skin. Cedar strips can be used to cauterize and bind wounds. Yet *Thuja plicata* demands respect; it can poison if ingested to excess.

"The cedar tree is 'every woman's sister,' because she provides for and sustains our existence," writes Haida lawyer and traditional performer Terri-Lynn Williams-Davidson. "She permeates every facet of Haida life, beginning in the cradle and continuing to the grave."

Indigenous and other careful users have harvested cedar sustainably for centuries. Then industrial-scale modern logging techniques ruthlessly gutted countless old-growth groves. Now there is a new enemy stalking our beloved trees, the human-caused extreme weather changes that threaten cedars' very existence. Are we now walking through a graveyard, amid the slow death of the mighty cedar in our coastal Galiano climate of drought and monsoon?

It seems unthinkable that the tree that cradled and sustained life in the Pacific coastal forest is now under threat. The harvest of cedar and its related uses—homes, boats, decking, saunas, and even flumes and chemical containers—still generates about $1.3 billion a year in BC. Its aromatic wood resists rot or corrosion and repels the elements as well as insects. Cedar seems like an unshakable constant in our coastal forests.

But today, cedar trees are literally drowning from drought. Their roots are so emaciated by ever-longer dry periods that they cannot capture or retain the moisture that drenches them every winter. Giant trees uprooted in winter's windstorms are dry and white as chalk at the heart of the root ball. Entire stands of cedar can be seen withering and turning brown.

BC forester Tanya Seebacher found that the "warm and dry summer climate" here markedly curtailed cedar growth and concluded "moisture stress may be the major determinant of redcedar dieback." Cofactors such as disease, exposure to air and ground pollutants, and overbrowsing by deer—destroying water-retaining undergrowth—further weaken the struggling cedar. And indeed the cedars can be seen to be dying back faster in hotter, drier areas and in more-polluted urban environments. Each year we have less rain on Galiano. Our air is choked with smoke from nearby forest fires during the summers, when chainsaws and other industrial machinery fall silent lest a deadly spark set alight a fire we could not outrun. It seems an alien environment for the classic image of a dripping cedar revealed through coastal fog. Nor can cedar easily adjust to the rising ocean levels and record king tides: it abhors standing with wet feet on the foreshore or in swampy wetlands.

Living as I do in the Anthropocene era, I feel like an ungrateful guest of the cedar that first welcomed me here and has sustained my life, guarding the ground where I restore my healing soul. After decades of writing about mostly Indigenous families whose sisters, mothers, and aunts have been grievously harmed, I came to embrace the solitude of gardening in North Galiano's rich yet acidic soil, surrounded by its tall cedar sentinels. The last wave of logging here rejected cedar as a non-commercial species; my elephant cedars are centenarians that have seen and survived so much of human life.

When I first came to live on the coast, forty years ago, my heart was bonded to the dry sage hills and willow/poplar forests in Alberta where I grew up, on a river island bordered with sandstone cliffs. One night on North Galiano, as I burned prairie sage and tobacco to offer thanks to my new home—as my father and Indigenous teachers taught me to do—the trees around me rose as if alive. I could suddenly see their great spirits as living beings. The dry prairie air was sucked out of my lungs and replaced by the sweet, sharp-smelling moisture of coastal cedar and fir. I felt welcomed to my new home after a childhood in the foothills where I felt safe and free mostly when I was outdoors. Drinking in the spicy cedar scent is now to me inextricable from my sense of home.

Plants cannot migrate like birds or animals, yet plant species can slowly abandon an ecosystem for one that is colder, wetter, or more hospitable. Or they can die out, to be lost forever. I recently traversed boardwalks in northern New Zealand to view breathtaking 2,500-year-old kauri trees the width of my kitchen wall and as tall as the cedars back home. Raised walkways and thorough shoe cleaning protect the kauri from the dieback disease that is carried in on the soles of visitors who come to see Tane Mahuta, a 2,500-year-old monolithic king of the forest, named for the Maori god of trees and birds. Will the cedars suffer the same fate, becoming relics in a tree museum? Or perhaps cedar will leave coastal BC to sustain human life in forests farther north. In either case, it would be a catastrophic loss.

So powerful has the cedar been on the West Coast that it has influenced human resettlement patterns. Maori and South Pacific Islanders are thought to have landed long ago on BC shores, forging family links now confirmed in the DNA of Indigenous families here. Vancouver Island's Nuu-chah-nulth people tell of Maori visitors who arrived in kauri canoes, stayed for years awaiting advantageous ocean tides, then returned in cedar ocean-going canoes. At the turn of the twentieth century, the Japanese came to coastal BC, including Galiano, following early reports of gigantic old-growth trees and abundant fish. Cedar must have seemed familiar to them; the Japanese sugi was also prized for its fragrant, healing properties and practical strength. On Galiano, the Japanese logged old growth, built charcoal pit kilns and salteries, fished, and exported a vast array of seafood. A village of up to four hundred people of Indigenous, Japanese, and Chinese ancestry flourished here until 1942, when the Japanese families were forcibly relocated.

Back then, cedar and other species like coastal Douglas-fir must have seemed in infinite supply to the Japanese. They burned trees in underground kilns to create charcoal, a valuable domestic and industrial fuel source. On Galiano, bricks of charcoal were shipped along a conveyor belt straight to the ocean and onto freighters.

At the north end of Galiano today, a tall cedar snag hosts eagles and ravens on the edge of deserted Saltery Bay, above what was once the bustling village. Three recent visitors from Japan, researching old Japanese kilns and villages, exclaimed how similar the BC coastal forests must have seemed to their ancestors. They admired the remaining stands of large cedar and the bonsai shape of junipers native to northern Japan. Not unfamiliar with species loss associated with climate change and pollution, they were deeply troubled by the cedar dieback they observed here.

To them, as to us, the loss of the western redcedar from coastal BC would be truly catastrophic. Is it too late to reverse the causes of cedar dieback, on Galiano and in other parts of the West Coast? For the sake of my elephant guardians, and all of the cedars' precious gifts, I hope not.

## Notes:

Terri-Lynn Williams-Davidson, *gi7ahl gudsllaay*, "Cedar Sisters" (2004). This statement is quoted almost every year in the Council of the Haida Nation's media statements, *Tllga Sii'ngaay Guudang 'Laa*, for Earth Day (April 21). Terri-Lynn repeated the quote in the Supreme Court of Canada in 2018, and it appears as words and song on her *Grizzly Bear Town* album released in 2017 (http://www.ravencallingproductions.ca/).

Tanya Marie Seebacher, "Western Redcedar Dieback: Possible Links to Climate Change and Implications for Forest Management on Vancouver Island, BC" (master's thesis, University of British Columbia, 2007), 102.

# More Perilous Than a Leaning Tree

**CHRISTINE LOWTHER**

What Bob McDonald means by *feedback loop*—
climate change is caused by deforestation,
deforestation is caused by climate change.

Canadian rainforests were not described at school.
We didn't learn of their existence
until years later in Pacheedaht territory
where we climbed trees, swam the river,
blocked the logging road with sticks,
boulders, fallen branches,
even dragged stumps from the clear-cuts,
made log-and-hammock tripods,
padlocked ourselves,
then threw on our shovels as the crummy arrived.

We wanted to keep candelabra cedars pitchforking the sky.

Back then we wore our fleece all summer
and called the second month Fogust.
Now it's Fire, smoke and sweat
as trees fall to greed and grief
before and after the solstice storm
that hurled down hundreds more,
opening the wind-funnelled gorges
to glare and sorrow and solastalgia.

Politicians want to prevent more fires
by pulling out the understorey,
turning Turtle Island's habitats
into lungless brown-mossed parks.
Overcautious arborists afraid of trees and lawsuits
climb into their dangerous trucks and drive.

# Futures on Ice

**JAMIE SNOOK**

---

When I was four, I fell through a crack in the harbour ice.

I was walking across the ice in Mary's Harbour in Southern Labrador under the watchful eye of two nans, one on each side of the crossing, when I suddenly disappeared into the water below. At four years old, I didn't know why there was water on top of the ice, or what it meant, and I probably was drawn toward it to play. Luckily, my coat was tangled enough above my head and caught on the ice, preventing me from completely sliding under.

All I remember is the shivering, the fear, the hot bath, and the frantic activity as everyone tried to save my life.

I was using the same route across the ice that I always took to visit my nan Snook. A straight path led from one grandparent's home to another, but there were blind spots and obstructed views. I am not sure who noticed that I suddenly fell through, but I know my uncle Ross jumped on his snowmobile and raced to my rescue.

I was lucky that day. Not everyone is this lucky where I live.

Another time, my family was going to William's Harbour, a small community in NunatuKavut territory, on an island, about thirty kilometres on snowmobile from Mary's Harbour. You would have to be from this place to know the conditions well. We did not, and inadvertently crossed bad sea ice. Several people from the community were on the hill watching the entire event unfold, praying for our safety. We all managed to cross safely and were quickly told about our poor decision. It's not entirely uncommon for people to take risks when crossing ice, but without local knowledge, the risks become uncalculated and more is left to chance.

We were lucky again that day.

Over my life so far, I have heard many other ice stories. Not all of them are so fortunate, and they highlight how precarious living with and relying on ice truly is. Many stories involving the sea ice are tragic, and people living in the North learn to respect ice and to be cautious on and around it. There are always conversations amongst community members before ice-use decisions get made. Today, information is often shared on social media:

*Michael:*
*January 26 at 9:04 a.m.*

Anyone down to Kenemich since last storm? What route did you take and what is going like?

    *Bridgett:* Brian was going down yesterday!

    *Henry:* Crowd went Burnt Point to Rabbit Island to Muldoons yesterday. Left at 3, got there 6. Bad drifting and soft snow and banky. Better to go Mud Lake road. Track was beat better. Some slush but no one got stuck in it.

    *Brian:* We came to Weasel Creek yesterday 2pm it was drifty and bumpy. Very slow going. I went to the Valley and back to Weasel 7pm and it was good going from Partridge Island to Shoal Point. Shoal Point to Seal Point was still drifty and bumpy.

Throughout my younger life there was no social media, but I would use the sea ice to visit friends in Forteau Bay or to explore the lands around my home by crossing ice. We would also use the ice to visit family farther north along the coast. On warm spring days, the sea ice was one of my favourite places to get a suntan, and large groups of Labradorians always used the ice for fishing, hunting, and travelling.

Every fall, I anticipated the freeze-up of the ponds and bogs so that we could skate. One pond that we used regularly always froze clear, and as we skated, we could see everything at the bottom. The water underneath was perfectly still, and it felt like the treasures of the pond were revealed. There was magic in those skating memories, along with a sense of freedom and well-being to play outside in our environment on our own schedules.

The Labrador coast is traditional Inuit territory, with Inuit and their ancestors living in the region for thousands of years. To this day, Inuit continue to rely on the ice extensively for travel and to hunt wild foods such as Arctic char, seal, polar bears, moose, and caribou. Just like people, the seals and polar bears are dependent upon the sea ice for reproduction, travel, and their own food sources and survival.

Inuit leaders have been communicating the risks of climate change for decades and, in particular, have been indicating large changes to ice throughout Inuit Nunangat: later freeze-up in the fall and earlier breakup in the spring; and when the ice does come, it's not as thick or as stable as before and doesn't cover as much area. There have been recent winters in Labrador when the ice conditions were poor. People can't hunt or travel as safely, and people experience fear and sadness about the way things are changing.

I have started to look more closely at climate change projections to see if I will get to continue a relationship with ice in my lifetime. I know from these projections that my connection will get progressively smaller each year as the ice patterns change, and that my children and grandchildren will not have the same opportunity to build a relationship with ice that I experienced.

Sheila Watt-Cloutier, a prominent Inuk activist, thinker, and global environmental advocate, articulates how Inuit rely on the sea ice for all aspects of life and culture, and that Inuit have a "right to be cold." Climate change is taking away that right.

Since the late 1950s, Labrador has been warming, with a snow season approximately forty days shorter in the last sixty years, and projections suggest that the ice cover season will be further reduced by three to four weeks by 2070.

In 2014, my partner, Ashlee Cunsolo, worked with Inuit in Nunatsiavut, Labrador, to create a documentary, *Attutauniujuk Nunami / Lament for the Land*, to share the stories of how climate change is impacting Inuit lives, livelihoods, and well-being. At the end of the film, Inuk Elder and leader Tony Andersen reflects on the changes to come. He says, "Inuit are people of the sea ice. If there is no more sea ice, how can we be people of the sea ice?"

I feel an increasing urge to make the most of ice while I can. I never feel the urge to leave my homelands and live in an ice-free climate. This year, I have used the ice more than ever. Ashlee and I have a small, unserviced cabin on the other side of Lake Melville, just north of Happy Valley-Goose Bay, Labrador. We can access it only once the ice freezes, so we wait with anticipation for the conditions to be good enough to cross safely.

This winter, we crossed Lake Melville several times a week. The ice crossing is always the most intense part of the journey, but often the most beautiful. Thoughts continually run through our minds about the safety and the thickness, the conditions and quality of the ice we are crossing, knowing what can happen if we have misread the conditions. But the ice also brings a sense of awe. And the ice brings us to places that we love, and every year we hope for good ice—ice the way it has always been.

Some weekends, when we arrived home, we were exhausted from the cold. It can take a lot of energy to stay warm when it is minus forty or colder combined with a wind chill. Our enthusiasm often brought us across the ice on days when most people would stay home, but there is further gratefulness that comes with a remote escape, wood fires, and the moonlight highlighting the black spruce.

There is a lot to be said for the freedom of ice. I think about this all the time.

## Notes:

Sheila Watt-Cloutier, *The Right to be Cold: One Woman's Story of Protecting Her Culture, the Arctic and the Whole Planet* (Toronto: Penguin Canada, 2015).

Ashlee Cunsolo, director, *Attutauniujuk Nunami / Lament for the Land* (2014), http://www.lamentfortheland.ca/film.

# What We May Understand

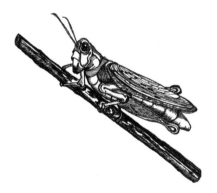

# All Our Relations:
# Climate Change Storytellers

**DEBORAH McGREGOR & HILLARY McGREGOR**

At 11:00 a.m. on March 29, my son asked me what time he was born. I was somewhat curious as he had never asked me this before. I told him he was born around 5:30 a.m. I realized then that I was not exactly sure what "born" meant in his question; he was a ten-pound baby and it took some effort to bring him into the world. I added that around 5:30 could mean more like 6:00, depending on what "born" meant. Then he told me his dream.

> N'gwis gii-bimose ziizabaakodokeng (My son walked into the sugar camp). At the entrance to the sugar bush, a trail runs about five hundred metres from the dirt road to the camp. Before my son set out along the trail he met a man, maybe in his thirties. My son did not recognize this man, but he knew he was from the North by his accent. The man told him, "The bees (*amok*), the bears (*makwook*), the trees (*mitigook*), the suckers (*nimebinwak*) are facing genocide, yet they continue to fulfill their responsibilities." He talked about suckers, that they are food, they are teachers, they keep the water clean, they fulfill multiple responsibilities, they face many hardships and suffer; yet they are not

complaining, they humbly go about carrying out their duties to Creation. These beings continue to do what they have been instructed to do; they continue to support the continuance of life through the sacrifice of their own. "Humans are not fulfilling their responsibilities," he said. "We are putting all life in jeopardy."

The dream was so vivid, so real, that my son did not know it was a dream until he woke up around 5:30 a.m. on his twenty-second birthday.

He was worried about what the spirit had told him. That humanity, by forgetting our purpose and responsibilities, will fail all life. He interpreted the words of the man/spirit as a call to action, to act on this message. However, the enormity of the task was overwhelming in light of the state of world.

―――――――――――

My son's name is Nenagahsang, which refers to what *aki* (earth/land) is doing at the time of year he was born: the sun is regaining some of its warmth; the snow and ice is beginning to melt. He was born during the Ziizabaakodoke Giizis (making sugar moon), a time when the earth is undergoing a transformation; it marks the end of winter, a change in order to bring forth new life. It is also exactly the time when *ziizabaakodaaboo* (sap) runs in *aninaatig* (maple tree). These are the trees that saved the Anishinaabek from starvation countless generations ago, by offering much needed nourishment when winter supplies were depleted. Nenagahsang also has another meaning: a person who is able to de-escalate a conflict or tense situation; to melt the tension away and bring calm to a situation. The name Nenagahsang is itself a gift, and speaks to his abilities.

I think to myself that there is something about the synergy of these events: the time of his birth and the dream, his name, the place, the moon he was born under—Ziizabaakodoke Giizis—the spirit visitor and the message.

The spirit's call to action has him troubled. That responsibility to act—what can one person do? It is not my dream to interpret, that work still has to be done. So instead I tell him the story of the Pipe and Eagle, the version relayed by Anishinaabe Elder Edward Benton-Banai in *The Mishomis Book*. In this story, despite teachings of how to coexist with the rest of Creation, and the gifts given to remind us (the *opwaagan, odeh'egan, semma*) of how to live, the people have become vain and unkind, and we begin to hurt each other and abuse our other relatives. The teaching of peace, humility, and generosity are forgotten, and the gifts are used to advance our own personal power. The Creator is upset about the abuse of the gifts that were provided to support all life. A spirit was to be sent to destroy the earth after four days. On the fourth day, just before the sun rises, Migizi (Eagle) calls to the Creator at *biidaaban* (at daybreak—there is already light), that very spiritual time when it is no longer night, but not yet day. The Eagle cries four times to get the Creator's attention and petitions to spare the lives of the people and the unborn. The unborn, the Eagle said, can learn from the humble few who still follow the instructions to live in harmony with the earth. It is the unborn that provide hope for the future and for people to correct their ways. The Eagle is thus entrusted with the responsibility to fly over the earth each day to find at least one good person who continues to live according to the principles of *mino-bimaadizawin* (living well with the earth—a good life) and report back to the Creator his observations. Each day, the Eagle seeks that one person or family about whom he can report back to the Creator so that life on earth can be spared.

There are many teachings in this story, but three come to mind. First, it is the Eagle who petitions on our behalf. We are not able to save ourselves as humanity, for despite our intelligence and our free will, we can choose to be destructive. Yet we are spared despite causing our own demise. Once again we are saved by our relatives (as we were by the *aninaatig*). Second, we have orchestrated our own destruction by our arrogance—we continue to ignore our responsibilities to life and the unborn. Third, the Eagle needs to find only one person still using the gifts as instructed to support life; if there is one person, one family, there is hope.

———

I reflect on where the spirit visited my son, at the entrance of *ziizabaakodokeng*, where my family has come together *minookming* (in the spring time) for countless generations to make maple syrup. Forest science tells us that in one hundred years maple trees may well disappear due to climate change. I cannot imagine what this means for generations to come, to not receive this gift from the *aninaatig* that was offered so long ago to nourish us in our time of great need. Despite all this, *aninaatig* continues to offer medicine water, year after year, despite increasing hardship, fulfilling its responsibilities.

It is easy to become disheartened, with climate change and other environmental crises threatening life as we know it. But then I remember the Eagle, who needs to find only one person to petition on our behalf so life will continue. So, year after year, my family continues *gii-miizhyaang* (to receive) from *aninaatig*, as we continue to nourish our spirit and pray that Migizi can find us.

These stories remind us of the tremendous yet often forgotten power possessed by our relatives, such as Migizi, *amooyak*, *makwook*, *mitigook*, *nimebinwak* and Aninaatig. These beings are wilful entities that can change the course of events in the minds and hearts of people and the rest of the natural world, both now and in the future. These stories remind us also that we humans are not the only climate change storytellers.

I suggest that the knowledge we need to survive as humanity may not derive strictly from the "human realm"; we need to revitalize and relearn the traditions that will ensure all knowledge is respected, including that from our relatives and teachers. We have not been able to solve the greatest challenges of our time on our own, despite great advances in science and technology. Human-centred and human-generated knowledge has not proven to be enough. Stories about what is happening now, and what *will* happen soon, are being told every day, every minute, by the earth itself. We have failed to remember the storytellers of the natural and spirit worlds; we have failed to listen to dreams, visions, and intuition. We need to remember that it is with *humility* that we must breathe life into our responsibilities and obligations to the continuance of life. We have to *act* on the stories being told by the earth. While it is often the voice and experience of the most humble that escapes our attention, we, like Eagle, must seek those who continue to support life.

# All on the Same Train: Bringing the Paris Agreement Home

**CHRISTOPHER CAMPBELL-DURUFLÉ**

## Le Bourget

The RER B train slowly abandons the platform, packed with formal attires from all around the world. The other travellers, slouched in their identical seats and longing to get home, raise their eyes to our head scarves, boubous, business suits, and ceremonial face paintings. We newcomers to the train car chatter with excitement, in loud smiling voices and myriad languages. Some are busy taking group selfies and exchanging laughs, while others write down email addresses to stay in touch. Hardly anyone looks behind at the Bourget suburb, and the rows of white police cars disappear out of sight in an impeccable send-off as we gain speed.

## La Courneuve–Aubervilliers

We ease into the next station and the rare passengers that get on look somewhat surprised. Not by our varied features or dialects; this area is probably as diverse as our group. But by how full the train can be at this late hour of the night. A tall and elegant newcomer will have to complete his journey standing. Who knows how many hours he has already stood today?

My gaze jumps from his lafa hat to the layers of tiredness accumulated under the eyes of the diplomats that fill the car. Two weeks of baguette sandwiches—*Tomate mozza ou jambon beurre?*—that disappeared too fast to feel like real pauses. Of Skyping faraway loved ones from hallways and cafeterias. Of parading in front of the military, who made us feel, despite their assault rifles and best intentions, like the Bataclan attack was going to happen again any time.

The RER winds through the high-rises and scrapyards. The "plenaries," "high-level segments," "contact groups," "action agendas," and "informal consultations" on the details of the draft treaty had lasted two long weeks. Before that, four years of preparation had lapsed since the Durban Mandate from COP 17, to negotiate a new agreement for the post-2020 period. And it had been another two years before that since the last time a concerted approach to respond to climate change had seemed to be within reach, in Copenhagen.

I can almost count the lines on the foreheads of some of my neighbours in the train like those on tree stumps: twenty-three long years have gone by since the United Nations Framework Convention on Climate Change was adopted in Rio. Many of those now swiftly rolling toward downtown Paris, unlike me, have patiently gone through the motions year after year.

## La Plaine–Stade de France

The RER doors open with a buzz on the stadium, a huge iceberg floating in the night. The December breeze whips our disparate group, and I imagine the eighty thousand fans cheering through the last minutes of the 1998 World Cup final.

Just like a few hours earlier, when Foreign Minister Laurent Fabius had emerged on the COP tribune before a crowd unsure of how the night would end. Perhaps naively, I thought that it was going to be another long plenary, where each negotiation bloc would read a statement of new demands for what should appear in the final version of the treaty. That delegates from highly vulnerable countries would go off-script to remind us how climate change is already affecting their home. Chad. Micronesia. Haiti.

This had been our routine for the past twelve days, after all. Each new intervention put another human face on the fact that high-emission populations like Canada's are dragging their feet. And each a stern reminder of the rule of consensus: if the objections raised persisted until the end, the whole process would derail. Then, just like after Copenhagen, we would have to continue facing climate change without a treaty. Like 197 soccer players on a green turf with no lines, and no referee.

## Gare du Nord

Some climate diplomats get off here and more people board the train. We are well within the city walls and start to blend in.

I was observing the plenary room from the back rows when Fabius returned. The negotiators suddenly became so silent that you could hardly tell their nationalities apart. Edna Molewa, South Africa's environment minister, who had been the spokesperson for the powerful G77 group throughout the conference, sat still and strong. One hand raised by her, one objection on behalf of those 134 developing countries, and work would have to be deferred to next year. Abdullahi Majeed, spokesperson for the Maldives. On his shoulders rested an enormous responsibility carried out on behalf of the Alliance of Small Island States: making clear to all those who use more than their fair share of the atmosphere that we are pushing some countries under water. John Kerry had also rushed back to his seat, an unmistakable grey fleck within a quorum that had so often lamented the United States's disengagement.

All were equally docile, despite huge underlying differences in climate vulnerability and diplomatic clout. Rumour had it that the Le Bourget conference venue was booked until tonight only, and that our microcosm would have to be disbanded, whatever the outcome.

As foreign minister, Fabius presided over this round of climate negotiations. Whether it was true or not, he had spent the two weeks repeating that the French team did not have an alternative negotiation text, and that each new version of the treaty—there had been almost one a day of late—was their best attempt at bridging positions. The metaphors made my head swirl, as "red lines" had to be respected, "landing zones" were (apparently) in sight, and "indaba" meetings (based on the South African negotiation technique) were convened night and day. It had seemed so detached from the people riding home beside me, and so utterly real at the same time. Behind each negotiated word, a story. Like that told by the Kichwa leaders from the Ecuadorian Amazon whom I had seen paddling their dugout canoe in the cold current of the Seine earlier that week.

## Châtelet–Les Halles

We stop again, one last time before crossing those same waters, which flow over nearly eight hundred kilometres from the eastern plateaus to Le Havre.

Christiana Figueres, executive secretary of the UN Framework Convention on Climate Change, had given Fabius a small gavel with the green leaf from the COP 21 logo in lieu of its head. It was there beside him, ridiculous but auspicious. He breathed in and dove into the text, his voice hoarse from tiredness, his eyes down, his round spectacles perched on the tip of his nose.

The Saudis could have leapt from their seat to request more safeguards for oil-exporting countries. Nicaragua also could have interrupted him, to request again that Europe and North America be bound to compensate countries exposed to climate harms. China could have interjected to request further assurances that the United States would hold up to its part of the deal. But everyone stayed put.

Hundreds of people were present from mountain ranges to coastal areas, metropolis to savannah, Arctic climates to Pacific Islands. NGO representatives, journalists, heads of state, researchers, company executives, and diplomats. All of us were suspended to Fabius's lips, at this timeless hour in Le Bourget. There seemed to be a shared recognition that something important could happen.

## Saint-Michel–Notre-Dame

More diplomats leave the train and disappear into the night. Those left on the car are discernible only by the blue UN lace around their neck. I wonder what thoughts inhabit their minds and incessantly replay the moment in my own.

Fabius read through a list of remarks in a matter-of-fact way— some of them were actually consequential last minute changes. He seized the tiny green gavel, and down it went on the podium as he declared the Paris Agreement adopted before anyone realized.

*Parties aim to reach global peaking of greenhouse gas emissions as soon as possible, recognizing that peaking will take longer for developing country Parties...*

People sprang to their feet and cheered, myself included.

*And to undertake rapid reductions thereafter in accordance with best available science...*

Some jumped and jumped again, some cried, most hugged their neighbours.

*Holding the increase in the global average temperature to well below 2°C above pre-industrial levels and [agreeing] to pursue efforts to limit the temperature increase to 1.5°C above pre-industrial levels...*

They rooted and shouted, revealing only then how afraid they had been during those two long weeks, how much they had doubted that this process could show a way forward after all.

*Recognizing that sustainable lifestyles and sustainable patterns of consumption and production, with developed country Parties taking the lead, play an important role in addressing climate change.*

They were so tired of fighting each other.

## Luxembourg

The RER B makes an exhausted sound as it stops under the regal park. The elegant man with a lafa hat was finally able to sit down and peacefully sleeps against the window. A teenage couple shares one pair of earphones opposite from me.

The chants still ring in my head, and I want to tell them how it happened. To ask what they think a world free of fossil fuels would look like. To confide how hopeful and tired and skeptical and afraid and excited I feel about writing my thesis on the new treaty. But the COP is over and the diplomats are gone, each with their version of what was achieved and what is still missing.

I just smile at them.

Implementation starts tomorrow.

# Left Behind

**DYLAN M. HARRIS**

---

I was eight years old that New Year's Eve. The weather was Mississippi cold, wet cold: the kind of cold that makes your bones feel heavy. I was at my friend Amanda's house, and we were playing with fireworks. She lived what felt like miles from the road, her home hedged in by pastures, ponds, and pines. We were full of hot chocolate and the chess squares her mother had just baked. I felt electric from the sugar.

It was getting close to midnight. Amanda, Dylan (another one), and I decided we wanted to try to fire Roman candles across the pond at one another, to see if any of the phosphoric pink flashes would make it. I was on the high side of the pond, so I had the advantage. The fluorescent sparks punctuated the still humidity, reflecting like lightning off the dark surface of the pond. None of them ever got close to crossing the pond, but it was still fun to try.

I checked my trusted Timex: 11:59 shone in Indiglo green. From my elevated vantage point, I could see over the pines. The sky hung full of stars. The condensation from my breath mixed with the caustic smoke of the Roman candle as I yelled to my friends that it was almost midnight. They put down their fireworks and began running toward me.

Midnight. My friends had not made it in time. Just as the Indiglo faded, I looked up, across the pines, and saw a streak cutting across the sky. It looked a lot like a Roman candle, but it was way too high in the sky. It was surreal. To my eight-year-old mind, the stars were always there, unmoving. To see one plummeting to earth at an impossible speed didn't make sense. My friends eventually made it up the pond dam, where they stopped beside me, hands on their knees, catching their breath. I turned to Amanda and asked if she had seen the flash. She hadn't. I began to panic. Somewhere along the line, someone had taught me that dead people lived in the stars. I knew that Jesus had died, and that he was supposed to come back at some point. The only conclusion I could fathom was that Jesus had returned to resurrect souls.

Worse, because we were all still there, we had been left behind.

I tried to explain what I had seen to Amanda and Dylan, who, after a few moments of me telling them we were left behind, were just as whipped into panic as I was. We ran to Amanda's house to see if her parents were still there, or if they had been tractor-beamed into heaven. It was a litmus test. They were good people. They went to church, and they actually enjoyed it. I thought to myself that, since I was left behind, I was lucky my parents didn't really go to church. They would still be around, at least until the seven-headed beast from the sea ate us all.

We got to the house and ripped the door open. We saw Amanda's sister first, asleep on the couch with the television blaring something from the Disney Channel. We rounded the corner and saw her mom washing dishes, humming to herself as if the son of God hadn't just skipped over her soul. Then we heard her dad rummaging around in the dining room. Apparently he was also unraptured, soul intact. In fact, he was totally normal. Considering how I had just encountered my fate of eternal damnation, something I had tried very hard up until that point to avoid, I needed normal. If her parents were still there, that meant that I was not left behind. Maybe Jesus was just checking in?

We yelled over one another into the hallway, trying to catch our breath and coughing from running in the cold. By the time we got her mom's attention, we all had tears in our eyes. We blubbered on about being left behind, about how I had seen Jesus streaking through the sky across the pond. Amanda's mom dried her hands on a towel. Then she explained to us what a shooting star was.

———

More than two decades later, I am still obsessed with the end of the world. I am not interested in creating it or bringing it about. I am not even interested in it as an end as such. But I have always felt drawn to it. As a kid growing up in a heavily Southern Baptist context, my obsession was invariably inflected by the Christian end of days. My favourite movies were about the apocalypse. It scared me, but I wanted to be close to it. I wanted to understand it. As I got older, religious connotations of the end of the days were replaced by other kinds of endings. I spent 1999's New Year's Eve huddled in a rain gutter in downtown Biloxi, Mississippi, while my mom and brother watched the ball drop. Y2K. In 2012, I spent the evening of the apparent end of the Mayan calendar sleeping under the stars on Isla del Sol, right in the middle of Lake Titicaca.

Most recently, I channel my anxiety and fascination with the end of days toward climate change, specifically with an eye toward climate justice. I have busied myself with organizing events, participating in marches, and adding to discussions, all directed toward enacting some kind of justice. However, throughout this work, I have grown bored with the tired, typical message of mainstream climate justice activism: that there are people to blame, and if you blame them harder, they are more likely to become more just. As someone who has thought quite a bit about the end of the world, I can say that, on the cusp of chaos, blaming doesn't go very far.

When I reflect back on my obsession, when I consider all of the ways I have tried not to focus on apocalypse and keep coming back to it regardless, I think I am drawn to end-of-the-world scenarios because they don't make sense. They are like a puzzle. They fundamentally challenge what it means to be alive: that time continues, that the ground beneath our feet is solid, that the air we breathe will always be here. Last-ditch efforts to save what you can, like in a house fire, abound.

Yet, regarding climate change, many worlds have already ended. In fact, the world we live in—the air we breathe—is a function of worlds ending. Multiple and ongoing extinction events pockmark geological history. Crises are nested into other crises, and oxygen is what is left behind. More immediately, however, social worlds have ended. Ways of life, different modes of planetary existence, have been upended time and time again. Considering how many worlds have ended through catastrophe and violence, however, just as many worlds have endured. They persist in the face of world-ending change and provide those of us still here with lessons about enduring in the wake of ongoing change. Rather than succumbing to being left behind, throwing hands up and into the void, we must consider the ways these worlds persevere.

For the better part of the last five years, I have been paying close attention to some of the worlds that persist in the face of climate change. Recently, I have listened to stories from folk artisans in Southern Appalachia who pick through the shifting landscape to harvest resources—berries and nuts—to make colourful dyes and pigments. The colours vary as certain plants disappear with the changing climate, but the practice, based on a deep knowledge of the landscape even in the face of change, persists. I have also listened to the complicated stories of coal miners, whose livelihoods are intimately tied to the changing climate. As pipelines move in, as mountain landscapes are carved to pieces, the miners increasingly understand their shared economic and climatic precarity. Their changing world tells stories, too.

In a world that doesn't make sense, a world that may conceivably be ending, listening to such stories is critical, because they help make sense of this world, as they always have. In many ways, I am still the kid who thought he was left behind. I still vividly remember the panic I felt then, and I often consider it deeply when I am confronted by increasingly dire reports about planetary chaos. However, instead of waiting for a seven-headed beast to eat my family, I think about climate change and about the worlds that endure despite, and in spite of, these changes. In reality, we are all left behind, and all we have are these stories. I like to think there is some kind of justice in that.

# Concerto for Scotch Broom

**CATRIONA SANDILANDS**

---

### Allegro precipitando

They say James Douglas himself in the 1840s carried in his pockets
seeds of Scotch broom to sow along the streets of Fort Victoria:
his vision of pastoral British paradise, built overtop
spacious Lekwungen-tended camas beds beneath the oak trees at
    *Meeqan.*

Eden secured by any means:
military or political, architectural, botanical.

The settlers around him, too, clothed their naked acquisitions
in bright-flowering Scots sentimentalities of thistle, broom, gorse.
Those less romantic (or less rich) saw in broom cures for dropsy,
for bleeding after labour. A source of dyers' yellows, greens and
    browns.
It was a brewer's fix in a place without hops,
that heightened both the bitter and the strength. And of course,
one could make a broom.

Broom came in the ballasts of the ships, cradled whisky
bound for single-minded prospectors,
spread through streams and rivers. It was deliberately planted
on roadsides, under power lines, to right catastrophes of soil.
It was a keystone in the building of a colony. It held together
        infrastructural dreams.

But broom has its own desires.

Its thousands of ripe, ballistic pods shoot seeds metres away,
summer after summer. (They can live, dormant, more than fifty
        years.)
Its waxy stems devour light even when it drops its leaves in drought.
It draws nitrogen from the air and roots in whatever scant soil.

They now say broom is aggressive, an invasive,
a competitor in the often dry, thin micro-regions of its flourishing.
That it is a fire hazard, that it is toxic and impenetrable,
that its roots are too tenacious, that it is (most ironically) an eyesore.

Up and down the coast run campaigns
to bust, blast, bash and blitz the broom,
to open ground for indigenous plants
in precious spaces like Garry oak meadows.

Where are the campaigns for giving back the ground
to the people who tended the plants and the fires
and made the meadows grow in the first place?

I have taken to saying that broom is a companion species
in settler colonial dispossession. It has also done its own settling
more successfully than anyone could have dreamed.

## Andante lacrimoso

the long slope of the hill
viewed from my front window
     is logged burned gouged
   shattered
   and alight with
      delicate leguminous
      yellow flowers
         awaiting bees

even new spring branches draw blood
resinous old bushes invite summer fires
elaborate root chemistries give rise only to grass

        and even the deer won't eat it (but
        I contemplate pickling the blooms)

extreme drought and rapid change
   favour global opportunists

      (like other travellers who wear
        prophylactic layers of gore-tex
          and bring their own freeze-dried food
      broom is an individualist with a sense of entitlement
       and little interest in friendly relations)

wet winter dry summer heat popping
     earlier blooming longer seeding
      accelerating timespace

changing climates assemble new neighbourhoods
    and we must learn
           eyes pods hands branches blood resin sweat
        mingling
to live in them.

       This busted land calls out in bright May blooms
        for deeper care, for story, for our love.


## Rondo con spirito

*damage has created novel ecosystems and the plants are slowly adapting*

scotch broom can be controlled mechanically
with a chainsaw (or at least sharp loppers)
at the point its main trunk appears above the soil

    *how we approach restoration of land depends on what we believe that*
            *land means*
    *land as sustainer land as identity land as grocery store and pharmacy*
        *land as moral obligation land as sacred land as self*

the plant will often not die on the first attempt and vigilant shearing
    is necessary

        *restoration is imperative for healing the earth but*
           *reciprocity is imperative*
        *for long-lasting successful restoration*

glyphosate herbicides are successful in killing broom
but the treatment must be applied before the flowers emerge

*we restore the land and the land restores us*

experiments are underway with biological controls
such as certain species of seed weevils whose larvae
enter the pods and eat the seeds before they disperse

*especially in an era of rapid climate change*
*species composition may change*
*but relationship endures*

cut broom in bloom
buy your Extractigator™ today!

*restoring the land without restoring relationship is an empty exercise*

**Notes:**

Troy V. Lee, "'Glistening Patches of Gold': The Environmental History of Scotch
    Broom (*Cytisus scoparius*) on Southern Vancouver Island, 1848–1950," BC *Studies*,
    no. 166 (Summer 2010): 39–54.
Italicized passages in "Rondo con spirito" are from Robin Wall Kimmerer, *Braiding
    Sweetgrass: Indigenous Wisdom, Scientific Knowledge and the Teachings of Plants*
    (Minneapolis: Milkweed Editions, 2013), 333, 328, 336, 337, 338.

# Such Good Friends

**SARA BARRON**

---

As a climate change researcher, I have steadfastly avoided one audience for my work: my own kids. How do I talk to my children about what we are facing? Do I want to reveal my sadness and fear to their growing hearts? When will they be ready for this conversation?

Unfortunately, the talk came earlier than I hoped. My eight-year-old son, Elliott, was on spring break from school this year, so he came to the urban forestry class I was teaching at the University of British Columbia. Elliott has been to my class many times, and it is usually fine: he plays Minecraft quietly in the back of the room while the class talks about trees. On this occasion, though, I overlooked the fact that the guest lecturer was there to talk about climate change and climate-adapted tree species. The speaker told us about deaths, both human and arboreal, resulting from summer heat waves. Fifty-four people last summer in Quebec, who did not have access to cool or shade. Hundreds of trees in our region, especially cedars—Elliott's favourites—that did not have enough water.

After class, on the way to pick up his little sister from day-care, out of the contemplative silence in the back of the car came a gentle question:

"Mom, are you worried about climate change?"

———————

Climate change is something I can't fully wrap my head around. It is too scary, too big. So, in forming my answer for my son, I reflected on the crutch I use for myself. To keep from despondency, I try to focus on a contracted issue, one that confronts the challenges climate change poses for us, but that also brings hope, perhaps the possibility of agency in the midst of the problem's enormity. For me, this issue is urban trees.

By and large, urban trees have the odds stacked against them. A cherry tree in our neighbourhood that we pass on our way to the park is pretty typical of the urban tree's situation. This tree is an Ukon flowering cherry, *Prunus serrulata* 'Ukon'. Its wide, gnarled trunk supports a relatively short and broadly spreading canopy that reaches halfway across the street and over the sidewalk. In spring, its clusters of pale, white-green blossoms fade to pink during its week of bloom. It is a relatively rare species in our city of eighteen thousand cherry trees. The Ukon cherry blooms late in the season, providing one last display of fresh blossoms before summer's heat comes.

As with most street trees, our cherry's roots are surrounded by pavement, leaving it without enough room to thrive. There are three trees along this section of the street, each likely over forty years old. Our cherry is isolated from its companions by a driveway. Its roots have heaved the sidewalk in many places, sometimes many inches high, in its quest for moisture and nutrients. The bumpy sidewalk beside the tree makes for a fun moment for the kids on their bikes, and so we often spend time near the tree. Occasionally, city workers try to manage the problem, shaving off the concrete or even re-pouring the sidewalk so that people won't trip. Inevitably, the tree's will to live prevails and the sidewalk heaves again.

I find hope in our cherry tree's resolve to live on the front line of climate extremes, but I am also cautious about its ability to survive in our future city. In the Pacific Northwest, predicted weather changes will alter water availability throughout the year: hotter summers will be coupled with longer summer drought and intenser windstorms, and rainfall will saturate soils, while milder winters will reduce winter snowpack and spring freshet. This year, the mild early winter in Vancouver almost decimated the cherry blossoms: they need a certain number of cold nights per year for optimal flowering. This trait evolved to prevent blossoms from opening before a late frost. Thankfully for the cherries, 2019 brought a record-breaking cold February, allowing our city to enjoy another *sakura* season.

After a long, grey, wet winter, two weeks of pink and white blooms filling the city are an awakening of spirit. But our Vancouver spring ritual of blossom "snow" in April may not be a certainty for much longer. Cherry trees are a good indicator of climate-related stress, as they require both summer moisture and reliable cold. Victoria is already experiencing dying cherry trees in the city centre as a result of climate changing weather patterns. Our cherry is holding on, but a few summers of drought have left it looking less vital than it once was.

Despite its uncertain future, our cherry tree is doing more than we are to mitigate climate change. Within its twisted trunk, the tree stores carbon. Every year, it absorbs a small amount of the emissions we create as a city. Larger trees absorb exponentially more carbon than smaller ones, which makes sense if you think about the sheer volume of leaf and branch found on mature trees. We need to protect the arboreal veterans in our cities. It might be appealing to cut down our middle-aged cherry tree, what with its pesky roots, to plant something more obedient in its place. We would mourn the loss of our friend. Even more urgently, we simply don't have time to wait for new young trees to grow.

A few years ago, our neighbour tied a swing to one of the cherry tree's strong limbs. The swing forges a bond with the tree that the kids can, quite literally, grasp. When we stop to try the swing, the worn rope and old boards bring challenge and focus to their relationship with the cherry. There is one huge root lifting from the ground that forms a step up and a place to push off your feet for the first swing. The top of the root is worn smooth and shiny from the neighbourhood children's feet lifting to the air.

Stopping at this tree provides a break from the fast pace of our lives, though I am often so rushed that I don't allow myself or the kids to really pause there. If I do, though, and feel the cool air beneath the tree's canopy, I feel like I can truly take a full breath. I spent my childhood in Stave Falls playing in the forest, learning which trees had the strongest limbs for climbing and swinging through hours of trial and error. Vine maple limbs were good for bouncing on, while alder branches tended to break. I discovered the latter one day when I was about my son's age. After attaching ropes and a board to an alder limb over a small stream, I sent my cousin crashing down into the mud on his first swing.

In the precious hours of my children's lives spent in the car every day, we are lucky at least to drive through urban forests. We were driving through one of them when Elliott, looking out at the blurred green, asked his question about climate change. I can imagine his big blue eyes registering a trunk or branch for a split second as the car drove by, a temporary blink away from his dream world. I wish that my children had more opportunity to climb trees: to wrap their small arms around trunks and branches, to use their toes to reach and grip as they pull themselves upward, testing the tree's strength along with their own. But this moment is better than nothing.

As I prepared to answer my son, I thought about the swing over the cherry tree's root, and that we should take a family walk to it tonight. I also thought about a movie we recently watched as a family. In Hayao Miyazaki's anime film *My Neighbour Totoro*, a story about two young girls' relationships with the spirits of trees, the father tells his children that "people and trees used to be such good friends." The film evokes some of the sadness of the lost relationships we once shared with trees. At the same time, it brings hope that the bonds can be restored. This is the message I want to share with my children. We have lost our connection, and continue to make mistakes, but there is still opportunity to once again be good friends with trees. If we can be friends, I hold out hope that we will find a way to face the new, difficult future together. Planting and caring for a tree, especially an urban tree, is a concrete contribution to forging friendship: a way to keep going forward in climate changing times.

I took a deep breath and answered Elliott's question.

## Notes:

I am aware of the contradiction involving a climate change story partially set in a petroleum-fuelled car. This choice was an intentional nod to the urban economy in which we must live and that we must confront daily in our personal and professional lives.

*My Neighbour Totoro*, directed by Hayao Miyazaki (Burbank, CA: Walt Disney Home Entertainment, 2006).

# Where Were You?

## CARLEIGH BAKER

> Clearly, we still do not understand the full consequences
> of what we did then because we are still inflicting
> major changes on the atmosphere. Then it was
> chlorofluorocarbons; today it is greenhouse gases.
>
> —Jon Shanklin

---

It was almost summer vacation. Tiff and I had spent Sunday afternoon prank-calling guys on the phone in my dad's study. Spinning in his leather chair and breathing the damp and spicy scent of pipe tobacco he stockpiled but never smoked. When that got boring, we yukked it up at the hand drawings of squishy naked people in the *Joy of Sex* book my parents kept on the top shelf.

At four o'clock, Tiff had tennis practice. We breezed past Mom in the kitchen, and I gave Tiff a Capri Sun juice to hold her through the walk to the leisure centre. She returned Mom's wave and gave me a wink.

"Byee, Jessie."

We air-kissed, because Tiff saw it in some European movie and said everyone here would be doing it soon. She had two sisters in senior high, so she always knew what was going to be cool long before everyone else. She always had the best hair: bangs that went nearly three inches straight up and cascaded into a churning wave of crunchy curls from her temples to her shoulders, where they softened a bit into a wash-and-wear perm. Held in place with scads of Aqua Net. We all used Aqua Net, because that's what our moms used.

"Byee, Tiffie."

———————

After the screen door snapped shut, Mom asked me how much hair-spray I thought Tiff used on her do. That's what she called it, a "do," and that made me think of beehives or bouffants or other ridiculous hairstyles Mom wore when she was my age.

I sucked on my Capri Sun and watched her grate cheese on the casserole, trying to figure out why she was asking. Behind her, the microwave clock flashed 12:00 in digital green. I knew exactly how much hairspray Tiff used because I'd seen her do it a million times, including touch-ups after gym class or an unexpected hard rain.

"'Bout a fifth of a can."

"A day?" Mom sucked in her breath, and I wondered if I'd some-how miscalculated the risk of sharing this information and was in trouble. For something. But what?

"Jess, do you know about the ozone layer?"

I shook my head. Something was happening, and it was Tiff's fault. Maybe my fault, too. Maybe everyone with good hair.

Mom put the grater down and sighed. "Well I don't know much either, not yet. It's in the sky. And it keeps the sun's rays from getting in and killing us all."

Of course, I knew the sun could be harmful. I put suntan lotion on in the summer, but not that lame fluorescent zinc oxide that Tiff said was only for teenyboppers. I'd never realized we had a built-in shield.

"What does this have to do with Tiff's hair?" I asked.

"Apparently the hole is caused by hairspray."

"Bull-oney."

She didn't seem angry that I sassed her, just a little bit glum, like she had other things on her mind. She pulled a newspaper clipping off the fridge and gave it to me. "HOW LONG DO WE HAVE?" the head-line said. I shoved it in the back pocket of my shorts.

"I'm going outside."

"Jess…"

"Ugh, yes, Mom, I have sun lotion."

I banged through the screen door and stood in the front yard. Shielded my eyes with my hands and looked up. The sky looked the same way it always did in the summer—the colour of swimming pools. Threaded with wispy clouds. What would a hole in the ozone look like? A tear into black space, with killer rays shooting through like lasers? Was there any way to close it? Seemed like something a superhero would have to do.

At least some of the answers must have been in my back pocket, but after standing there for a while, all I could think about was how happy the sun made me feel. Just a minute or two with it on my face and I was smiling, thinking about long lazy vacation days at the beach. How can a person possibly worry about the weather when it's like that?

A familiar truck drove by slowly and the passenger whistled at me. Todd Smits. "Nice ass!" he yelled, like he didn't see it every day in class. Brian Green was driving. He was older than Todd, in senior high. "Where's your friend?" he called.

Gag me. I waited until they were down the street and flipped them the bird: something Tiff would do. Brian's truck lingered at the stop sign and I wondered if he'd seen me give them the finger, but eventually he took a slow left and disappeared. I sat my nice ass down on the lawn, wishing there was a suntan lotion to make me invisible.

———

The next day, in science class with Tiff, I found myself staring at her hair. I'd noticed she was trying an even more ambitious do than usual. It was a trophy, something that set her apart from other girls. And people took notice: the guy who did the school photos had spent extra time on her, getting the lighting just right, he said. "Looks like carved wood," he kept saying, swishing his hands around her head until she rolled her eyes at me. She laughed, and I laughed too, loud, until the principal poked her head in the room and told the photographer to get on with it. Good hair was truly a blessing and a curse.

We weren't learning about the weather, but I raised my hand and asked Ms. Simpson about the ozone layer anyway. She pushed up her glasses. "The ozone layer is between fifteen and thirty kilometres above the earth's surface. Ozone is created naturally when oxygen molecules..."

I waited for her lips to stop moving so I could get to the point. "But is hairspray destroying it?" People laughed. Tiff kicked me under the table, and I wondered if she thought I was making fun of her.

"Hairspray." Ms. Simpson blinked. "The problem is chlorofluoro-carbons."

"In hairspray?" Tiff said.

"Chlorofluorocarbons are fully halogenated paraffin hydrocar-bons produced as a volatile derivative of..."

Ugh. Why don't science people ever just answer your question?

After class Tiff was all over me. "Just because you're jealous..." She tossed her hair.

---

"I'm not, my mom just said..." I reached into the pocket of my shorts but I'd washed them last night, dissolving the newspaper clipping.

A hand closed over mine. "Yep, your ass is still there," Todd Smits said, grinning like an idiot. My body clenched at his touch, but I smiled back. Guided his hand away.

"Still there," I said. Todd kept smiling, and stupid Brian Green peeked out behind him to make eyes at Tiff, and it was obvious we'd been selected as summer romance delegates by these boneheads. I'd barely said a word to Todd that year, and neither of us ever talked to the senior high guys. So why us?

"Gross me out," Tiff said, and they stomped off, cackling like crows. Tiff elbowed me in the ribs. "Did he touch your butt?"

"Yeah."

"Ew. Come with me," she said.

The light in the basement girls' washroom was terrible for makeup, but hardly anyone ever went down there, so it was quiet. We pulled out our bags and went to work, relining lids, dabbing pressed powder on jawlines. The bell rang, and we ignored it. Tiff pulled out her hairspray and went to town, the mist around us growing so thick we had to breathe through our mouths so we wouldn't sneeze and screw up our mascara. I watched little dust particles find each other in the air and cling together.

When we were done, we just left. It wasn't the first time we'd ditched. It was only four days until the end of the year, and most teachers had checked out anyway. The sun beat down on us, and Tiff talked about the zipper-front bathing suits she'd seen in an Italian magazine her mom read.

"Gonna be hot this year," she said.

Zippers sounded uncomfortable in the sun. "Bring the magazine over and show me tomorrow."

We took the long way back to my house, waiting for three o'clock just to be safe. Mom was out but she'd left cookies. I picked at one while Tiff went to use the bathroom, but she called me in, laughing. I asked her what was so funny and she pointed at the counter. The Aqua Net had been replaced by a pump-action bottle, something called Ice Mist. It looked expensive, like it came from an actual salon instead of the drug store. A sticker across the top said CFC FREE, with a little happy face.

"She's really worried about that ozone layer, hey?" Tiff said, spraying the Ice Mist and recoiling as it came out in a heavy stream. "This shit is never gonna work."

"I guess she is," I said. "Moms are such boneheads."

"Total boneheads. Hey, what are we going to do about Todd and Brian?" Tiff said, pulling her brows up so they arched dramatically.

"Dunno." I didn't want to tell her that the only thing I felt was ashamed. That I hadn't yelled back that afternoon on the street, or slapped Todd when he touched my butt. The whole thing felt weird. "Do you like Brian?"

"Dunno." She pursed her lips and sucked in her cheeks, flirting with her reflection. "He's okay."

"What happens if we don't like them?" I said, trying to sound breezy. The wheels were already in motion, whether I liked it or not. What could I do?

"Dunno," Tiff said. Sun spilled in the bathroom window, and the AC kicked in with a low rumble. Somewhere out there, our protective coating was wearing thin, and I suspected Ice Mist wasn't going to be enough to fix it.

## Note:

Jon Shanklin, quoted in Robin McKie, "Thirty Years On, Scientist Who Discovered Ozone Layer Hole Warns: 'It Will Still Take Years to Heal,'" *The Guardian*, April 18, 2015, https://www.theguardian.com/environment/2015/apr/18/scientist -who-discovered-hole-in-ozone-layer-warns.

# Scale Model

**SONNET L'ABBÉ**

---

## i. Nation

When a group of us, concerned about climate and water, start to talk about the anthropogenic nature of the changes we're seeing, about the impact of human activity on the planet, Stan bristles. "The impact of *some* humans' activity on the planet," he corrects.

We come home and bathe our children, filling up a whole bathtub with water that gushes, potable and hot, through the taps. A capful of bright pink stuff under the stream magically makes white clouds of rose-scented bubbles.

I write a poem about the bleached coral reefs. I write a poem about fish farming and wild salmon populations. I write a poem about ocean acidification and scallops. I write a poem about the rising tides and the escalating height of waves crashing on the west edge of Turtle Island.

In Sumatra, a decent "bathroom" is a tiled space with a drain in the floor. In one corner, the squat toilet's hole is framed by flat, ridged ceramic. In the other corner, in the wall at knee height, there's a basic spigot. Beside the spigot, a red plastic bucket. In the bucket, a couple of litres of still water. And a red plastic ladle, floating.

Extreme heat and drought turn watersheds to cracked earth. Cape Town anticipates Day Zero. They turn off the taps in public washrooms and set bottles of hand sanitizer on the counters. People line up to fill plastic four-gallon jugs at water stations. People keep their showers to thirty seconds. Then a bit of rain comes and Day Zero is pushed to next year. Some suspect it was all a PR ploy to get South Africans to reduce water consumption. Some South Africans, I should say.

In the Parliament Buildings, there were once no restrooms for ladies. In the Parliament Buildings, at one time, none of the restrooms were accessible. In the Parliament Buildings, thirty-seven bathrooms are now gender neutral. In the Parliament Buildings, the old stalls are beautiful, with shining brass hinges, and doors made of broad sheaths of grey and white Italian marble.

"Water Is Life," say women walking down Commercial Street, carrying a banner. "Water Is Life," say a couple who came down from Unist'ot'en, at Koksilah, in the high-ceilinged room of what used to be a "school." There's a protest on Burnaby Mountain, near a lake and tents. Johnnies-on-the-spot stand bright blue and erect on a patch of grass. Flows of awareness, in the Peace River, in the tailing ponds, in my every-morning gold stream.

## ii. Community

As long as the snowpack returns,
> we capture winter precipitation up at Jump Lake Dam.

As long as the seasons stay stable,
> we hold water until the summer, when Nanaimo's demands increase.

As long as the rain comes,
> we release water downstream to the South Fork Dam, built in 1932.

As long as the streams are full,
> we bypass some water to the Nanaimo River, to ensure fish habitat and recreation are preserved.

As long as the snowpack returns,
> the water destined for taps flows by twin pipelines.

As long as the seasons stay stable,
> it flows using no energy but gravity, to the South Fork Water Treatment Plant.

As long as the rain comes,
> all water flowing to Nanaimo passes through filters in this state-of-the-art facility.

As long as the streams are full,
> we filter particles down to one ten-millionth of a metre.

As long as the snowpack returns,
> we produce water that is clear, fresh, and very safe to drink.

As long as the seasons stay stable,
>    water flows from the Plant through pipelines to reservoirs
>    around the City.

As long as the rain comes,
>    we reserve critical volumes of water in reservoirs, for
>    unforeseen demand or firefighting needs.

As long as the streams are full,
>    we deliver drinking water through more than six hundred
>    kilometres of pipe networks.

As long as the snowpack returns,
>    we test water hundreds of times per year to ensure its quality.

As long as the seasons stay stable,
>    the system will make boil-water advisories a thing of the past.

As long as the rain comes,
>    the Water Treatment Plant can handle up to 117 million litres
>    per day.

As long as the streams are full,
>    we can supply enough drinking water for more than
>    150,000 people.

As long as the snowpack returns,
>    we would like to thank James Johnny for the metalwork.

As long as the seasons stay stable,
>    the Raven, the Salmon and the Man Within grace the entrance
>    to the facility.

As long as the rain comes,

    they remind us the Snuneymuxw First Nation contributed

                        $500,000,

       and helped the City

                        acquire

                   Crown

                             land.


As long as the streams are full,

    reserve #2 will now have access to clean water.

### iii. Planet

Ocean, sister water.
Ocean, fluid in the amnion
                    of atmosphere.

     Our brothers
     have been marrying ten-year-olds
     since unmemory.

Wash, wash
the dirty laundry,
the dark stains in cotton picked
by my body,

our brothers
banished the moontide red
        consciousness
          from the sanitary
                neighbourhoods.

~

Ocean, hushed
as a thunderous

rush of adrenaline, hushed
as the little
flush of rage in
a woman

pushed just a little bit,
 pushed just a little bit,
  pushed just a little bit,

past her
comfort zone.

~

Ocean, absorbing
the dioxides
of decision, decision, decision

      ocean of saying nothing

      ocean of saying nothing

absorbing the heat
    of human

           othering

      acid-
   ification
stomach-
    ing

      us

~

It comes out in the pH.
It comes out in the hard rains.
It comes out in the detention centres.
It comes out in the harsh winds.
It comes out in the drought.
It comes out in the stillbirths.
It comes out in the hurricanes.
It comes out in the tent cities.
It comes out in the floods.

~

Ocean, so
emotional.

Our shallow
self-regulations
ripple
through you.

You say nothing,
but your tenderness
melts icebergs.

They roll down
your cheek
in fifty-foot waves,

wiping
city shore-lines
from our eyes.

# Our Bodies, Our Wetlands

**ASTRIDA NEIMANIS**

As I shut the car door and step out onto the gravel, I notice the used condom at my feet. Places like this have long served as settings for unsanctioned desires: unmarried sex, queer sex, paid-for sex. I take a photo of this morning-after souvenir and head out to the viewing platform.

Windermere Basin is located at the tip of Hamilton Harbour, along the highway that stretches from Toronto to Niagara Falls, the latter made famous as much for its heart-shaped honeymoon hotel beds as for its natural wonder. About an hour into the drive, you hit the Skyway Bridge as the lake opens to your left and Hamilton's infamous industrial skyline rises up to the right. The Basin is almost under the bridge, in the southwest armpit of the lake.

It's easy to miss. If you take the Eastport Drive exit, though, and pull into the mostly empty lot that announces a small park, you might find me at the end of the short walking path, standing on the concrete slab that overlooks the Basin.

I'm drawn here by other love stories: ones that arise between humans and vegetal, elemental, and animal natures. We are drawn together by our messy exuberances and shared vulnerabilities in this climate changing world.

It is difficult to imagine that this place was once a natural wetland and mud flat used mostly by Anishinaabe and Haudenosaunee people. Colonization and the industrialization that followed made this environment unrecognizable. Thirty years ago, it was one of the most polluted bodies of water in North America. Choked by sewage flowing in from the Red Hill Creek and heavy industrial deposits from Canada's biggest steel industry, it was considered an ugly and polluted cesspool.

Today, the field is bursting with goldenrod, and a fish jumps impossibly high from the creek waters. The Basin is located on a seasonal bird migration path, as a hawk's shadow moving across the scraggly weeds reminds me. This is part of the reason why, in 2002, Hamilton launched a $22 million remediation plan to restore part of the Basin to marshland. New dikes are accompanied by a fishway, three small artificial islands, birdhouses, and the short track that brought me to this platform.

Windermere Basin is now one of Canada's largest inland wetlands. Official reports claim that it is "healed." But what does this mean? The park remains crammed between highways, junkyards, factories, and a sewage plant. It is loud and smelly. As industrial poisons have started to settle down, climate change is stepping up: temperatures climb, cyanobacteria bloom, and water levels fall to reveal unstable, toxic muck.

Still, I am in a strange kind of love with the Basin. The air is sultry, yet the tall grasses are moving, alive against my legs. Purple and orange flowers insist on glamour despite late-season seediness. Everything here is trying to figure out how to persist. Somehow, we all sense that persisting will be better if we can find new ways to give ourselves over to each other's half-broken presences.

I no longer live in Hamilton: I moved to Australia four years ago. When I visit, I come here to experience these queer pleasures, but also to think about what I have inherited and usurped. I am a white settler woman made by these waters, but I am also complicit in their making.

Hamilton's waters flow into the Great Lakes watershed, an area covered by the two-hundred-year-old Six Nations Dish with One Spoon treaty. Passing around a dish of beaver tail, each party to that agreement would take only what they needed. I've probably told that story incorrectly, but I think it is my responsibility to try to tell it, in acknowledgement of how we settlers have failed it.

The lives of those who have belonged to these shores much longer than I start to surface. I think of that used condom, and then about all kinds of love, sex, and kinship that have been suppressed by settler colonial norms. I also think about young women, and cars, and deserted parking lots, and sex, and the vastly different ways these stories end.

It feels a bit disconcerting to be so smitten with this place. There is something dirty and sexy and a bit unkempt about Windermere: all that squishy mud and panting vegetation, sticking to your palms and up your nostrils, the tickle of a caterpillar moving up my bare arm, the blissful warmth of the polite Canadian sun in September on my closed eyelids.

At the edge of the parking lot I pass a pile of broken furniture and empty beer cans, evidence of a different kind of morning after. From the viewing platform, I look down to the creek waters pushing past. Although most of the industrial slag has been capped and sealed, the waters still carry the overflow from the waste-water treatment plant. The bank is thick with water bottles, shotgun shells, stir sticks, candy wrappers, coffee cup lids, Styrofoam, straws, and Kinder Egg toy casings.

I climb over the platform railing to examine the shoreline trash. A cormorant is moving strangely in the water, flapping as though about to take off, but then repeatedly rolling over to one side. As I move closer, I see it is snarled in fishing line. I take a stick and tangle it into the line to pull the bird closer, and then, having nothing else with me, I chew on the nylon until the bird is free. It paddles away slowly, but the line must still be wrapped around its wing. Although it keeps trying, it can't take flight.

As I walk away, an inchworm makes its way slowly across the gravel path. Swallows swoop in formation. Yellow butterflies cut the breeze with their winged cursive. Carp move like stealth craft through the murky creek, whose surface swirls with the chartreuse ejaculation of early autumn pollen. I begin to understand that although climate change is called the "sixth extinction," these devastating extinguishings are also, strangely, about desire, exuberance, and proliferation.

The lives and deaths hastened by climate change help me think about desire in more capacious ways. My desire is to still belong to this place, to experience the heady pleasures I find in the company of all this itchy fecundity. But I also find desire in the remnants of settler consumer capitalist appetites now archived in these waters.

My eye is particularly caught by the proliferating rainbow of plastic tampon applicators. All of these menstruating bodies are turned inside out, flushed down the toilet, to later arrive on the mucky bank of this inland sea. I am reminded that these bodies are reproductive bodies. We desire, have sex, and sometimes make new humans.

But in this climate changing world, the meaning of reproduction must expand. Blue-green algae flourish as the waters warm, while so-called "invasive" species like the round goby thrive in the effluent, all precipitated by the specific coming together of these waters, these histories, this climate, at this time. Reproduction is also about reproducing certain institutions and ideologies in these waters: reproducing the ability of corporations to externalize damage, or reproducing the settler colonial understanding of water as dump.

And what of water's own reproductive capacity? All living bodies of water—mammals, birds, reptiles, fish, insects, plant life, fungi, bacteria—owe their existence to gestation in a watery milieu. Water itself is a reproductive body, yet these wetlands are heaving under the petrochemical, disposable, climate changing weight of our dumped desires. Our love affair with the good life reproduces itself in these waters, but what happens to water's own capacity to make new life? What happens to water's own desires?

Although I am baffled by all of those tampon applicators, we shouldn't blame the menstruator. We should instead challenge a sex-gender system that keeps a menstruator's intimacy with their body shameful. Flushing a plastic applicator means we don't have to touch ourselves, or admit that we have bodies that bleed, desire, and maybe even make other bodies. The reproduction of shame also swirls in these waters.

Climate change has been called "everything change," but we might also pay attention to what gets reinforced in its wake. Reproduction, here, means asking: What thrives, what is altered, what persists, what is destroyed, what is constrained?

I look down at the metal handrail that wraps around the viewing platform. Someone has scrawled with permanent marker: *Wish you were here.* These words confirm the inadequacy of Windermere's "healing" and remind me of all that is disappeared and damaged: birds vanished in a tangle of fishing line, attempted colonization of Indigenous sexual worlds, a debilitation of water's own reproductive capacities.

But these words also make me alive to everything that still persists. The presences and absences, the extinguishings and exuberances, are *both* reproducing the future. What relationships—perhaps unsanctioned, relegated to dodgy places and denigrated bodies—will become necessary for new kinds of flourishing and desire?

# The North Saskatchewan

**LAURIE D. GRAHAM**

I don't want to write it. I know the scene as home:
the oil refineries rising from poplars

overlooking the river, the tank farms downstream,
the off-gassing from stacks painted like candy canes,

the manufactured cloud formations—
they treat their flames as eternal, eschewing the clean

for the cheap and the quick. I don't want this
tied to the trees or spoken aloud,

this inheritance, our confluence, our shame,
the windows of the houses on the opposite bank

observing the transfers, the neighbourhood park
that used to be the dump, and the quiet

of the river through each process, the banks
dropping away slowly, the river so large and old

it's assumed both impervious and already dead,
but instead it's eroding the ground, and for good reason.

No footpath, no worn shortcut across the park.
Bicycles sounding like trains across the wooden bridge.

Anything edible here I never did know.
The taste of grass in the mouth, the feeling

that doing this searching might kill me.

The birds soaring high over the river,
the grasshoppers, the grass making a feeling

in the back of the throat.
People alone parked under trees.

Refinery giving way to ravine, giving way to
river. The refinery's chainlink resolute, lining one side of the trail.

If one could encroach with seeds,
blow a dandelion over the line.

Dragonfly hovering, the bank
receding, their chainlink in danger.

The smell of thistle, the sweetness of an open field under sun.
Sky and ground, half and half, flag of Ukraine.

The roses, the raspberries, the human
scale. A soccer field comes into view.

The massive rumble to the east
always there, can't be ignored,

but as you get closer to the road
your attention must turn toward it.

# To the Post Office and Back

**PETER HOBBS**

My mum needs to mail a letter and we decide to walk to the post office located in a nearby 7-Eleven. She is quick to set the tone:

"This town is covered in dog shit. You can't go for a walk without stepping in it. I've always hated it here and wish we had never moved." My mum has lived in Sarnia for about thirty years, and while she regularly disparages the town, she is also steadfast about spending the rest of her days here. "At this point of life," she states, "I can't imagine living anywhere else."

Mum's house is in the south end of town, within walking distance of Imperial Oil, just one of the sixty-two refineries and production plants that inhabit the region. Most of these homes were built in the postwar boom of the 1950s to house a growing workforce, and as we move down the block, we're guided by a strict but comfortable cadence that reverberates on both sides of the street to form an echo chamber: two-storey bungalow with white wood and aluminum siding, blacktop driveway, detached garage, green cut lawn: *da capo*, return to the beginning and repeat. This pattern is punctuated with large maples, elms, and draping willows. There is also an abundance of cedars, known for their ability to suck up ambient toxins, such as cadmium, mercury, and lead.

Located in southwest Ontario, Chemical Valley—which includes Sarnia—is one of the biggest concentrations of oil production in North America. The constant stream of grey clouds billowing out of the smokestacks that line the Riverside Parkway constitutes a palpable ideology, one that literally floats in the air. The priority here is to "crack" crude oil, to transform the fossilized remains of prehistoric life (mostly cyanobacteria, plants, and dinosaurs) into desirable hydrocarbons, such as different types of fuel, rubbers, plastics, and pharmaceuticals.

In charting the petropolitics of Chemical Valley, it is crucial to foreground Aamjiwnaang, the Ojibwa First Nation of around 850 people that sits in the middle of Chemical Valley, surrounded by these oil refineries and production plants. This proximity is no mere coincidence. Much of Chemical Valley has been built on land that was part of a vast Ojibwa treaty reserve that has been steadily gnawed away by a series of shady private sales and government appropriations. In 1829, when Treaty 29 was signed, the Aamjiwnaang reserve encompassed 10,000 acres. It is now approximately 3,100 acres. This orchestrated land grab is a prime example of how the petroleum industry works with various levels of government to perpetuate a not-so-subtle form of white settler colonialism.

Mum and I pass the ambulance depot and she reminds me that the main reason she stays in Sarnia is that she is afraid of losing her memories of Jim, my stepfather. My brother Mike and his young family live in the small town of Corunna, just south of Sarnia, and there has been some talk of my mum moving there. "I know I would be happier if I lived closer to your brother," she says, "but I don't want to give up my independence and all the things here in the house that remind me of Jim. But then again, a day doesn't go by when I don't relive his death." She tells me again how Jim came back inside from having his morning smoke and grasped his chest. How she watched helplessly as he collapsed and hit the kitchen floor with a loud thud. How he was in tremendous pain as he struggled to get his breath. And how he was dead when they put him in the ambulance.

As we move down the block, our conversation drifts from general comments about the weather to the wildfires in California. Mum surprises me by bringing up the subject of climate change. "You don't have to convince me that temperatures are rising," she says. "Even your uncle Bruce believes in global warming. He might've voted for Donald Trump but he's not completely stupid. He knows that when we were kids there were four distinct seasons and now we only get freezing cold and sweltering heat. But today we got lucky. There is a breeze to help cool things down." We also review the various British murder mysteries we are currently watching on Netflix. This is a reliable subject that both my mum and I go to whenever we struggle to find things to talk about. We land on the subject of Sherlock Holmes and we agree that Jeremy Brett's queeny portrayal of the bachelor detective is by far the best. Mum and I rarely speak about me being gay. She never asks if I'm seeing anyone. So I take her acknowledgements of both Brett's performance and global warming as minor victories.

At the top of the street we are overtaken by a wave of benzene, a sickening, evergreeny smell that quickly engulfs us (imagine holding a bottle of Pine-Sol in front of your nose). In chemistry textbooks, benzene is celebrated for its elegant simplicity and versatility. There are competing histories of how this popular synthetic was discovered, but the most common story involves the nineteenth-century German chemist Friedrich August Kekulé having a recurring dream of Ouroboros, the snake eating its own tail. One night, Kekulé dreamed of six snakes joined together to form a six-sided bond. On waking, he immediately went to his lab and synthesized a six-strand molecule. Benzene, the resulting hydrocarbon, eventually became an all-purpose compound that found its way into a variety of consumer products, many of which are known for their aromatic properties.

Along with aftershave and air fresheners, benzene has been used to make such common items as Aspirin, plastic coffee cup lids, and Lego. It is also a well-known carcinogen. Today, one of its primary uses is as a lubricating agent. Benzene is injected into the gooey bitumen of the tar sands so it can travel through pipelines and be refined to produce more benzene, which in turn can be injected into the gooey bitumen. Another Ouroboros. Another echo chamber.

Both the benzene and the dog shit are reminders that smelling is an involuntary act in which we become aware of a smell only after it has entered our bodies. Picture the benzene and dog shit molecules entering our noses. Those that make it to the roof of the nasal cavity are absorbed by the sensory neurons in our olfactory system, which set off a chain of signals that our brains then use to identify the smell. While this seems straightforward, it is important to stress that the benzene and dog shit are moving through our nervous systems long before we can react. Even if we manage to avoid stepping in shit because we have been given the advance warning of its smell, it is already part of us. Benzene is harder to avoid stepping in, as it evaporates into air very quickly, and you can only start to recognize its smell when it reaches 60 parts per million (ppm) of air. A five-minute exposure to high levels of benzene (10,000 to 20,000 ppm) will kill you quickly. Long-term exposure to intermittent lower levels of benzene may kill you slowly. It is particularly associated with acute myeloid leukemia (AML). According to a 2016 government report, refineries in Sarnia release about three to ten times the annual "safe" limit. Aamjiwnaang is still waiting (and pushing) for a comprehensive study of the health effects of their intimate relationship with benzene and other chemicals.

On the way back from the post office, Mum surprises me again by asking a direct question about my research. "What do you mean by chemical intimacy?" By echoing my words, she gives me a gift: apparently, she has been listening to my rants about petropolitics.

Not wanting this opportunity to slip by, I respond quickly: "Petrochemical products are everywhere so that it is next to impossible to envision living without them. They are intimately part of our lives, and places like Sarnia are left to live with the toxic fallout."

Mum remains silent so I feel compelled to add a further point. "I mean, think about it: mothers pass toxins on to their infants. Just as mother whales transfer poisons accumulated in their bones and tissue, human mothers offload some of their toxic burden onto their children through their embryonic fluid and breast milk. When we're born, we're always already a bit DDT, PCB, lead, plastic, plutonium, and benzene. Talk about intimacy."

As usual, Mum has the last word. "Well, I hope you're not blaming me. I should remind you that you were a breech birth. You may have inherited some DDT, but you made up for it by causing me hours of excruciating labour." We smile at one another. I have heard this story before. And as we turn up the driveway, Mum asks if I want a grilled cheese sandwich for lunch.

# Running in with a Word

**PHILIP KEVIN PAUL**

Those who say
*It's pissing out there!*
Must have forgotten
We're made mostly of water.
As in Saanich now
That we've learned poverty
And that Mr. Clean is better
Than having dirt in one's home,
We must have forgotten that
We were made of tears
And earth.

Then those who say
*Canada* mean the continuous
Verb, *stealing*?
As *civilized* means
To cut down forests
To wipe mustard from
The corners of one's mouth.

In the little school building
Where nuns beat children
With wooden paddles
And bundles of hay wire,
My old people made a refuge
For our language.
It was perhaps the first act
We'd witnessed of such, as taking
A word and trying
To shove a new meaning into it.

So when our old ones were also becoming
Our *weary ones,*
After running through their memories
And the homeland of their childhoods,
Where now there are private properties
And the streams are ill,
What an astounding breakthrough
That the eldest of them all
Came running in to the old
School house without her cane,
Shouting KEKE,WÁTEN, KEKE,WÁTEN!
*That's what we called it,*
Meaning that little animal
They call a grasshopper now,
That little animal that seemed to know
Its desirability was its unattainability,
At the onset of summer,
But seemed to surrender
To the soft small hands
when the days were cooling again.

# What We Imagine

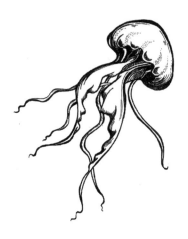

# Grow Pumpkins on My Grave

### LOIS BEARDSLEE

When I die, if there are people out there who care about these
    things,
Please place pumpkins on my grave.

So that beautiful, fanning leaves find moisture in drought,
Wilt under stress, only to recover, and spread green and joy
Radiating out and away from my memory and teachings

So that beautiful, ribbed vines and tendrils find open space all
    around the periphery of my loved ones,
Bearing protective rasps and gentle green hairs
Radiating out and away from their yellow-blossomed wombs

So that sun and shade may alternately nurture my families' tests
    and trials,
Smooth-skinned youth and hard-shelled maturity,
Bearing thick scars and dark moles that testify to protective
    melanins and genetic diversity.

When I die, if there are people who still honour seeds of future
   generations,
Please place pumpkins on my grave...

Not the pale yellow ones that came from corporate storehouses,
And overwhelmed the old ones with cross-pollinated threats
Against future generations of tenuous and fragile fruits that
   nurture our tomorrows.

Plant the bright red and green pumpkins from my childhood
Whose blossoms flavoured our winters with micronutrients steeped
   in forevers,
Whose seeds yielded proteins for our bodies and souls to become
   future pumpkins and eaters-of-pumpkins.

Plant me small, large, and convoluted pumpkins that sing of wild
   flavours and textures,
That hang drying dipped in sweet, tree-blood syrups that my loved
   ones harvested
From riverbanks and sunshine and sacred microclimates thick with
   always.

When I die, if there are people who still know about these things,
Please bury me under water-borne sands...

Sands smooth and clean to the touch, once immense and fearless
   stones
Standing where waters meet to lovingly grind away at strong, hard
   resources
And distribute their mineral strengths to radiating tendrils and
   hungry grasses

Sands roiling and singing loudly with gravity-generated songs of
    generations
Thriving wildly in moisture's plenty and deprivation's lessons,

While ever-present winds blow hot and cold with alternating gifts
    and challenges,
Sands carrying memories of villages and families thriving in the
    openness of confluences,
Where sunlight and openness yield respite from throngs of growth,
Competitive, crowding life forms, hungry neighbours grasping for
    rich sands' various strengths.

When I die, if there are people who still honour the regeneration of
    hope and persistence,
Please bury me under water-borne sands...

Where the only rainbow oil slicks come from decomposition of
    luminescent microorganisms
That feed upon fragrant oils from sinews and fibres of aspens and
    algae
That fed upon the muscles and tendons of the predictability that I
    radiated outward toward my loved ones.

When I die, if there are people who still know how to do these
    things,
Please weave my long soft hair...

Among the silky fibres of drying inner barks of life-giving cedars,
Once tall and teasing the sky with busy, upward red and brown
    fingers,
In anticipation of sharing their strengths forever as confluential
    waters fled their aging bodies,

Among the busy fingers of women weaving survival in double-
strand strength,
Twisting away, pulling toward themselves with competence that
comes from knowing how
To intermingle the strengths and weaknesses of alternating forces
into fibre monoliths,

Among the soft-nest caresses of tiny birds who feed hawks and sun-
loving snakes,
Where my feet have pressed seeds from sweetgrass and pollens into
green spouts
Emerging from the fecundity of mucks and muds that held
regeneration in temporary respite
from rapid waters and constant motion.

When I die, if there are people who still want to do these things,
Please weave my long soft hair...
Among the lives of my loved ones at the confluence of history and
destiny and infinity,
Always long-legged and eager for survival where sands become soil
and water is science and physics,

Tugging away at gravity to create resonations sung by my families
to soothe precipitation into wide lakes and seas.

# Five Ways to Talk about Twisted Oak Moss

**HOLLY SCHOFIELD**

## With the Usual Authority

Among the seven hundred mosses in coastal British Columbia, twisted oak moss—*Syntrichia laevipila* (alternatively, *Tortula laevipila*)—is a meek and unassuming member. An indicator species for degradation of air quality, it can be found in small and scattered colonies struggling to survive in the coastal areas of northwestern North America.

Associated mainly with Garry oaks (*Quercus garryana*), themselves unwilling bellwethers of the effects of stronger winter winds, twisted oak moss wraps thin but protective green blankets around oak trunks and limbs, as if to stave off the inevitable.

Its leaf clusters, less than three millimetres high, are infolded and twisted when dry, but spread out when moistened, tapering to rather elegant points. Setae—sporophyte-carrying stalks—tend to bristle among the diminutive rosettes, tiny reddish spears defending their home.

## With a Child's Innocence

"Where's the twisted oak that the moss grows on?" my niece asks as I hold her small fingers and guide her along a trail carved across one of Galiano Island's steep hillsides by tourists on dirt bikes. Tall invasive grasses slap their seed heads against her sunburnt cheeks.

The moss is what's twisted, I say, as we pass our first tortured oak, bent under the strain of many pressures. While Garry oak trees in the Gulf Islands may eventually benefit from climate change due to hotter, drier conditions, the associated ecosystems that include twisted oak moss may not.

My niece enjoys helping me hunt for the moss here on the island. With endless hope, she points out vibrant green mats of mosses and lichens, none remotely similar to our quarry.

I tell her where to put her feet to reduce hillside impact and to avoid crushing queen's cup and rattlesnake plantain. I talk to her of ecosystem processes and show her the Fibonacci spiral in an acorn cap. Her eyes light up and I describe other biomimicry—synthetic spider silk, solar paint, ceramics based on seashells—each the result of thousands of years of human observation. In the less diverse world that looms ahead, what will stimulate our future solutions to our survival?

I point to a bare outcropping and recall a recipe from a brochure. "How'd you like to make a moss milkshake?"

"Yuck!" Her dismay at such a beverage changes to delight when I explain how some mosses respond well to mixing with yogurt in a blender, then being poured thickly over rock, coating it. The spores in the capsules will inoculate the boulder with new moss colonies.

We carefully collect a small handful of the very common glittering wood moss (*Hylocomium splendens*). I tuck it in my pocket for later.

## In Its Absence

Later that summer, I tread down a narrow fir-crowded path and enter a Garry oak meadow, a kilometre from the one where I'd taken my niece. Juncos, robins, and even the wasps grow quiet at my presence.

The nearest Garry oak, surely more than two hundred years old, is a likely location for my target. I squat down amid invasive Scotch broom and pull out my hand lens. Although difficult to distinguish from look-alikes without microscopy, twisted oak moss does become more recognizable under stress, producing a great many offshoots. I'm unsure of my identification skills, but that proves immaterial: no miniature petal-like leaves of moss clad this tree.

Bees circle then land near my elbow on the brilliant yellow of yet another invasive: tansy ragwort. Far down the cliff, deer rustle amid swordferns as they browse on the frond tips, not a normal food for them; so very many deer, overpopulated by the eradication of predators and longer, drier, grassier summers.

I tell myself my search is a hobby, part of my participation in an eco-tracking website. I know it's really for my comfort: to establish this bryophyte's presence will reassure me that our increasingly less complex world still has enough functioning components. Does the disappearance of one species matter? More and more, we discover that such losses have a ripple effect far beyond what was first believed. The eradication of passenger pigeons in eastern North America in the late nineteenth century changed those very robust ecosystems much more radically than was first thought.

I watch an ant cross my boot toe, marching over a fallen oak branch that bears gaunt, shrunken bark, a branch that will linger for decades before rotting.

Beyond, where meadow meets forest, another small oak tree wends its way skyward, partially shaded by a sun-hungry arbutus. A tufted greenish blanket wraps its lower trunk.

I step carefully past stonecrop and sedum. I kneel.

It's only an immature specimen of *Ceratodon purpureus*, red roof moss, one of the most common mosses in the world, common partly because of its ability to tolerate high levels of air pollution.

I stand with aging, aching knees and head for the next oak, this one even deeper in the shadows.

## In Hul'q'umi'num'

On Galiano, the Indigenous Hul'q'umi'num' language (shared among Penelakut, Lamalcha, and other local peoples) has a generic word for moss—*q'uts'i'*, a sound as soft and mild as the bryophyte itself—as well as more descriptive names based on location and appearance. Curious about traditional Coast Salish uses, I do a quick internet search. Although twisted oak moss has too-short leaves and too little absorbency to have been of value, the sphagnum species were of vital importance: Diapers. Menstrual pads. Scouring pads. Decorations. Berry storage material. Steaming material for camas bulbs. Fish-wiping material. Caulking for longhouses. The list is long but details are few.

In my search window, a link for a traditional Snuneymuxw story catches my eye.

I click on it.

In *The Great Blanket of Moss*, as told by Celestine Aleck, Mother Tree's saplings insult Snow, causing Snow to threaten them. Mother Tree attempts to apologize for her children, to no avail. The Creator tells her to turn herself into a blanket of moss and wrap around her children, providing them with nutrients and protecting them from cold. Her children lament the change in their mother and learn how their offence has injured other trees. They eventually apologize to Snow, but the environment is forever changed.

The many layers in this story intrigue me, and I realize that my compiled list of "uses" is only a very small part of what moss has to tell us.

## In the Quiet of My Mind

Three months later, I lie in yellowed fall grass near a bare oak trunk. With eyes half-closed, I imagine the bark quilted in twisted oak moss, imagine the moss's travel through time.

Season after season, it grows and tastes the air. Tiny setae ripple and empty their caches, scattering microscopic spores into a great vastness, unseen but no less real.

The oak expands outward, its trunk fracturing in two directions under the strain, a chessboard of thickening grey squares.

Slugs trundle past, sticky with the rich detritus of the forest. A fairy slipper grows nearby, then collapses and browns. A deer grazes amid hundreds of types of ground cover. A lone human strides by, clad in woven cedar clothing, intent on other forage.

A century passes. European colonists arrive, so many colonists. The ozone thins, dark skies storm longer and colder, deer hoofprints deepen. The meadow crumbles under careless boots and dirt bikes.

Then, a careless cigarette is tossed.

Although Garry oak meadows are fire-adapted to the less intense fires historically set by Indigenous Peoples and those occurring from lightning strikes, current human-caused forest fires are far more destructive, burning with such intensity they can reduce a meadow to nothing but ash and bedrock.

How long can twisted oak moss hide from fire? From sour breezes that float particulates over from BC's mainland? From destruction by far too many deer? From increasingly fierce winter storms?

I didn't find twisted oak moss that day or any day since. Is it uncommon on Galiano or simply overlooked? There is only a sole entry on the local eco-tracking website. Inconsequential and ignored, the moss's rarity continues to be unknown.

My observations as a citizen scientist are squeezed into a busy life. My attempts to educate my niece are haphazard. Local Indigenous knowledge systems transform with every generation due to external forces (much like ecosystems everywhere). Complex district bylaws, formed with good intentions, often don't succeed in protecting rare species. The local conservancy makes a courageous effort to shield Garry oak meadows from trampling picnickers and deer but can do nothing about increasing summer temperatures or catastrophically hot forest fires.

Such scattershot methods of conservation are not enough. People now outnumber the Garry oaks on Galiano.

If twisted oak moss vanishes from this intermingled ecosystem we call Earth—an ecosystem that includes us—the outcome may be minimal. Or it may be a cascading effect that will become clear only after years of study.

And that's the real issue.

We simply don't know.

When we decide we do need to listen to twisted oak moss, will it still be here?

**Note:**

Celestine Aleck, *The Great Blanket of Moss* (Nanaimo, BC: Strong Nations Publishing, 2016).

# Ocean

**ANN ERIKSSON**

---

Law school hadn't prepared Gina for jellyfish. The blades of her oars churn through a swill of translucent orbs that dip and tumble, over-turning in the wake of her stroke, their long tentacles streaming after like hair. All those thousands of hours in the library, hundreds of books, and years of lectures with no mention of these free-swimming marine animals. No one, not a professor, a fellow student, her arti-cling supervisor, had described how to navigate her way through an army of cnidarians.

She drives the blades through the crowded water and cringes, wondering if she's hurting them. These ones are white with round yellow centres, two, maybe three hand spans across, like oversized fried eggs, their tentacles as fine and pale as vermicelli and as long as her arm. She breathes in. No odour from the jellies, just the sharp brine of the sea. Yesterday afternoon the surface lay thick with purple-red angry bruises, and in the morning, transparent white-blue moons the size of butter plates that seemed to glow with an interior light. Too many to count.

She stops rowing and leans over the gunwale. How many fathoms down do the fried-egg jellyfish go? Layer upon undulating layer until it becomes too deep for her to see. For two days she has been rowing through nautical mile after nautical mile of the ethereal creatures. She'd sailed *Osprey* right into the flock (or was it herd? school?) before she realized they were there. She had dropped the sail and watched the spectacle for what must have been an hour before she took up the oars and tried rowing through them.

She wishes Forrest could see it. Her son loved anything to do with the ocean, anything about nature, really, but the ocean most of all. Took after his grandfather, Forrest did. He was always wet and bringing home treasures he'd picked up from the beach or netted from the waves. Sea stars, crabs, clams, sea slugs he told her were nude branches. She couldn't remember all the names. His room had been crowded with saltwater aquariums that Nate had helped hook up with hoses and a solar pump. At least before the sea life began to disappear. How quickly it happened. Most of it gone from one year to the next.

Gina wants to dip her finger into the sea and touch the jellyfish but she knows their tentacles are armed with stingers and she can't remember how dangerous they might be. Forrest warned her the tentacles of some species could kill a full-grown person writhing in agony, but it was her marine biologist father who had predicted the wholesale takeover of the ocean by hordes of jellyfish, which would thrive in the warming, acidifying waters. *When nothing else is left, there will be jellies*, he'd said to her and Forrest one day while out in *Osprey*, not long before he died.

The hull is slipping backwards in relation to the shore, backwards with the jellyfish or the current or both. She resumes rowing and the oars slice through the mass with a swoosh, tumbling the few in the path of the blades. Everything she knows about jellyfish came from Forrest. *Sea jellies, Mom. Not jellyfish.* She can still hear the affection in his ten-year-old voice as he scolds. *They're not fish, you know, Mom.*

She squints south through tears, as if she can conjure her son out of the distant haze that hangs above the waves. His mop of sand-coloured hair, those earnest grey-blue eyes, ears too big for his head, a mouth that never stops talking, story after story, so many, so detailed and lengthy she tunes out. His hand on hers as he points out the underside on a lion's mane jelly washed up on the beach, the lumpy orange sacs like gelatin that she thinks must be gonads but, he tells her with authority and a touch of annoyance, are the creature's mouth. *They breathe through their skin.* She wonders if he's taller than she is now, and if he still wakes up in the night and calls for her. She hopes his sister comforts him.

Gina stops rowing again, frustrated at the lack of headway, tips the oars out to rest on the gunwales, and wipes the sweat from her brow with her forearm. She stretches her fingers, then closes them into a fist, opens them again and turns her right palm up. A blister shines through the cracks in the leather of the cycling gloves she'd thought were such a good idea.

From the bilge, she retrieves the flask of water she'd desalinated that morning. The first sip makes her flinch, her lips dry and cracked from the unrelenting sun and the salt air. She's lost count of how many times her skin has peeled from her nose. She takes a second drink, another, then drags the shade tarp from the bow locker, drapes it over the boom and secures it. As she works, she wonders how Phoebe's body might have changed in the time she'd been gone. Her daughter's fifteenth birthday is coming up. She'd have her period by now. Those sprouts of breasts... Gina can't let her mind go there. No mother to answer the all-important questions, to celebrate the markers. As if Phoebe would have asked any of those kinds of questions, ever wanted to celebrate such things with her mother. Phoebe, the sullen, quiet one with the judgmental eyes and the secrets. Ever since she was a toddler. *What's in your hand, Phoebe? Where are you going? What did you do at school today?* Her answer: a toss of her head, a tight-lipped scowl, or a gaze aloof with intrigue. *Nothing. Nowhere. I'll never tell.*

Gina traces the knife cuts she's made each morning on the edge of the seat. Twenty-three days since she and *Osprey* left the shelter of Dolphin Bay and the uncertain sanctuary her family and the other refugees from the floods and fires had created there.

Gina wishes Dieter was with her. He taught her to sail. Together they built *Osprey* from a set of plans mailed from England. Five metres at the waterline, her hull teal green, red gunnels. They'd trailered the sailing dinghy from the city to the cottage at Dolphin Bay and launched her the first day of Dieter's retirement. Now *Osprey*'s wood is faded from weeks of constant exposure to salt and sun, the pale blue sails thinning with wear. The opposite of Gina, the skin of her face and hands thickened and darkened to a cinnamon brown. Inside, she's feeling as beat up as the boat.

Dieter would have known what to do, how to make headway through the damn crowded sea. His last words to her, uttered as he left on a rescue mission from which he never returned: "When you know something, you must act on it." If her father had lived, if the flood hadn't taken him, she wouldn't be floating in a soup of jellyfish somewhere off the coast, weeks from home, not sure where she was headed. He would have kept his grandchildren safe.

The memories of her children from the day the *Providence Sun* had sailed into Dolphin Bay, and changed all their lives, have travelled with her and *Osprey* like two following gulls. Forrest and his exhilaration hurrying her out of the garden and through the village, down the hill toward the beach to show her the ship newly arrived in the bay. His slight body, swooping and jumping and twisting, a kite on a string, and her a rock, holding him to the earth. If she let go of his hand, she'd sensed, he would float up and away on the wind, leaving her behind.

And Phoebe, standing in the shallows, farther out than the other children, up to the tops of her thighs in water, the skirt of her sundress wet to her waist. Her hair hung loose to the middle of her back, errant strands floating about her head and lit by the sun like a golden aura. The girl's body strained toward the ship, her arms raised, one crooked to shade her eyes, the other lifted in greeting.

"Phee," Gina had called out, then louder, "Phee."

Her daughter's narrow shoulders had pivoted, her budding nipples pressing through the thin damp cotton of her dress, her hips turning too, her feet still planted in the direction of the open ocean. Her lips had turned up in a smile, but her gaze remained distant with a longing that Gina had at the time interpreted as rapture at the sight of the radiant ship, but now recognized as the first sign of her departure.

A thump sounds on *Osprey*'s hull. Then again, followed by the slap of waves on the starboard topside. She leans over and looks down, then reels back at the sight and the smell of a dead sea lion, a young one, bloated, its flesh falling away in pink chunks, revealing angry yellow puss-filled pits. She pulls up the collar of her T-shirt with one hand and covers her nose and mouth, and, with the other hand, grabs an oar and pushes the sea lion away and back, so that the swollen body rolls around *Osprey*'s stern and drifts off, rocking in the chop. It's not the first dead marine mammal she's encountered. Wherever the jellyfish flourish, she sees them, as if the water was poisoning them, or they'd starved, finding nothing but jelly slime to eat. She can count the number of living birds and marine mammals she's seen in the past three weeks on one hand. It's creepy, the silence, the absence of life. Where are the schools of fish from her days sailing *Osprey* with Dieter, the bow-riding dolphins, the whirling flocks of gulls, kittiwakes plunging into the waves to feed?

The shade tarp gives a sharp flap in a rising breeze. Her heart lifts at the promise she can stop rowing. But which direction should she sail? The telltales on the rigging tell her the wind is blowing onshore where the coastal cliffs soar darkly, mirage-like, the surf sending up a spume of white at the base. All around, in every direction as far as she can see, the bell-like bodies of the fried-egg jellies open and lift, then close, open and lift, as rhythmic and as graceful and silent as ballerinas, tugging her steadily north, back toward Dolphin Bay and Nate. The opposite direction of her children.

*When you know something, you must act on it.* She takes down the tarp and stows it in the bow, then drops the centreboard to full, hauls the sail, and sets the jib.

"Sorry, fellas," she calls out to the jellies, then grabs the tiller and pulls in the sheets. The sails fill with a whoosh. *Osprey* jumps to life, surging through the mass of brainless, gutless, translucent orbs, parting them in a tumbling swath. She sets the sails on a close reach to counteract the tendency of the wind to push *Osprey* sideways toward the cliffs. Or at least she hopes that's what will happen. Never captain, always crew...until the night she rowed alone out of Dolphin Bay in search of the *Providence Sun* and her children.

The sturdy little sailing dinghy surges forward through white-capped waves. Clouds spill over the horizon, the sky an angry charcoal grey. The air temperature drops, heavy with moisture. She lashes the tiller and sets out her rain-collecting bucket, then digs out her one sweater and her foul-weather gear. Lightning flashes. What had Dieter taught her about lightning? Head for shelter? She glances behind her at the receding cliffs, then ahead into the unknown. She tests her safety harness with a tug, tucks a handful of dried apples from her dwindling supply into her pocket, then hunches over the tiller, waiting for the storm to hit, heading south.

## Note:

This story is excerpted from *Imagine*, a novel-in-progress.

# Key to the Conifers of Galiano Island, 2150

### LAUREN MAGNER & ANDREW SIMON

Conifers are among the most ancient of living seed plants, having evolved on Earth about 310 million years ago. Their waxy leaves are well adapted to harsh conditions both dry and cold, a trait that has allowed them to proliferate throughout the world. Conifers have thrived in the Northern Hemisphere especially, by virtue of their ability to retain leaves through winter. Hence many conifers are commonly referred to as "evergreens." In this region, however, the term evergreen periodically does not seem to apply, as many species wilt and turn brown every summer in response to seasonal drought. Cast in the rain shadow of the mountains of Vancouver Island and the Olympic Peninsula, Galiano Island's already dry summers make the island particularly vulnerable to the rising temperatures entailed by climate change. The severity of summer drought is such that even the most iconic conifer of the Salish Sea, the western redcedar (*Thuja plicata*), is now in decline.

Climate change impacts on Galiano Island's horizon include sea level rise, extreme winter rain events, and increasingly severe summer drought. At the more dramatic end of the predictive spectrum, several of our conifer species might eventually vanish. A more probable outcome, however, is a restriction in their local distribution and abundance, while those more resilient become more prominent. With these potential impacts in mind, "Key to the Conifers" imagines people in 2150 learning to identify these trees in the dry, semi-Mediterranean climate of Galiano Island, BC, using a set of technical keys. The dichotomous format of the keys serves as an aid to field identification of species based on contrasting botanical features. To use these keys, you would compare the traits contrasted in each numbered couplet (1a versus 1b) with the tree in front of you and then, on deciding which of the options applies, follow the lead to the next nested couplet. Eventually, each lead in the keys resolves in a species account considering potential fates for each conifer, invoking signs of stress already seen in 2019.

Written in the formal style of a botanical flora, adopting both Western and Indigenous nomenclature, these keys are as much an artifact of a colonial past as they are a guide for an unknown future. How will these conifers appear before us a century from now? How will we recognize them and call them by name? Whose names will we use and what knowledge systems will guide us? These are some of the questions that lie between the lines of the following keys.

## Key to the Conifers of Galiano Island

Trees evergreen, bearing scaly or berry-like cones ............... 1

**1a** Leaves needle-like, alternate or occurring in clusters along branchlets ........................................................ 2

   **2a** Leaves occurring in bundles or fascicles of 2–5 needles each
................................................ *Pinus* L. 3

     **3a** Leaves occurring in fascicles of 2–5 ................. 4

       **4a** Fascicles of 2 leaves; common along Galiano's NE coast ............................. *Pinus contorta* Douglas ex Loudon **Shore pine**; trees aspiring to 15 m tall, with crowns rounded in profile; bark grey-brown; cones 4–6 cm; once limited in extent to the northeast shores of Galiano, this species remains marginal in distribution but has been favoured in areas subject to recent wildfire, its contorted branches often swollen with resin masses caused by red turpentine beetle (*Dendroctonus valens*); called qʷənəɬp in Hul'q'umi'num', a name that generally refers to "pine."

       **4b** Fascicles of 2–5 leaves; naturalized .. *Pinus ponderosa* Douglas ex C. Lawson **Ponderosa pine**; trees seldom attaining 70 m in height, with blackish bark becoming cinnamon red when mature; cones 8–14 cm; a species introduced as a legacy of forestry, occurring in homogeneous stands, now naturalized and locally abundant in areas subject to recent wildfire; due to extreme rainfall in winters, however, its growth remains stunted; a tree with no name in Hul'q'umi'num', elsewhere it is called *(s-)ʔápɬqʷ-az′* in Stl'atl'imx (Fraser River), *tsiɬtsiɬ*, *tsiɬ* in Tsilhqot'in, and *sʔétqʷɬp* in Secwepemc.

**3b** Leaves occurring in fascicles of 5 . . . . . . . *Pinus monticola* Dougl. ex D. Don **Western white pine**; seldom 80 m tall, with thin grey bark becoming plated with maturity; cones 15–25 cm; a sparse yet resilient population limited in distribution to Galiano's coastal bog ecosystem; many snags stand in the bog, testament to fluctuating water levels caused by beaver activity, blackened by wildfire and surrounded by regenerating saplings; called *t'thqéʔəɬp* in Hul'q'umi'num', or *qʷ′əqʷ′ayíʔləshəɬp*, meaning "dancing tree."

**2b** Leaves not in fascicles, alternating along branchlets . . . . . . . 5

**5a** Defoliated twigs rough to the touch . . *Tsuga heterophylla* (Raf.) Sarg. **Western hemlock**; a graceful tree with a drooping terminal bough; cones green to brownish, 1.5–2.5 cm; mostly limited in distribution to the understorey of mixed forests where seedlings establish on decaying "nurse" stumps; where this species has assumed a dominant position in the canopy as a result of logging, trees now dying back and subject to wind-throw due to their shallow roots; called *t'ᵗʰthqínɬp* in Hul'q'umi'num'.

**5b** Defoliated twigs smooth . . . . . . . . . . . . . . . . . . . . . . . . 6

**6a** Leaves sessile (without petioles) . . . . . . *Abies grandis* (Dougl. ex D. Don) Lindl. **Grand fir**; needles spreading horizontally; cones light green; trees once grand, to 90 m tall, and common in mixed forests throughout Galiano; now stunted and dwindling in distribution, largely restricted to the understorey of mixed forests along the northeast coast of the island; windstorms have toppled many of these trees in more exposed aspects; called *t'áʔxʷ* in Hul'q'umi'num'.

**6b** Leaves with petioles . . . . . . . . . . . . . . . . . . . . . . . . . . . 7

**7a** Leaves obtuse; cones hiding mice . . . . . . . . . . .
. . . . . . . . . . . . . . . . . . . . . . . . . *Pseudotsuga menziesii* (Mirbel) Franco. **Douglas-fir**; seldom attaining 70 m tall, with coarse, brown bark, resistant to fire; cones proliferating following years of extreme drought, borne at the tips of previous year's growth; a common, drought-tolerant species, it remains the most prominent conifer on Galiano, though its productivity is here much restricted; many trees exhibit black scars, scorched by wild-fire; a resilient tree, it is called *ts'sey'*, for "wood" or "log" in Hul'q'umi'num'.

**7b** Leaves acute; cones red and berry-like . . . . . .
. . . . . . . . . . . . . . . . . . . . . . . . . . . . . *Taxus brevifolia* Nutt. **Western yew**; 5–10 m tall, with thin bark exfoliating to reveal reddish-purple inner bark; a species particularly sensitive to changes in light and temperature, occurring infrequently in the understorey of older forests in cool, moist north-ern aspects of the island; its strong, stiff wood is excellent for making tools; called *təxʷátsəɫp* in Hul'q'umi'num', meaning "bow tree"; the Latin *Taxus* also refers to the bow.

**1b** Leaves scale-like, opposite or whorled . . . . . . . . . . . . . . . . . . . . . . 8

**8a** Leaves scaled or needle-like; seed cones berry-like; strictly coastal . . . . . . . . . . . . . . . . . . . . . . . . . . . . . . . *Juniperus maritima* R.P. Adams **Seaside juniper**; shrubs to 10 m tall; juvenile leaves needle-like, long persistent; limited to marginal coastal environs where it establishes on water-shedding rock outcrops; its distribution has become restricted locally due to rising sea levels; called *p'at'thənə́y-eɬp* in Hul'q'umi'num'.

**8b** Leaves evenly pleated; seed and pollen cones scaled . . . . . . .
. . . . . . . . . . . . . . . . . . . . . . . . . . . . . . . . . . . . . . . . . . . . *Thuja plicata* Donn. ex. D. Don **Western redcedar**; trees to 70 m tall, buttressed at the base; bark reddish brown, pliant, and easily stripped; fronds bronzed and wilted in summer; increasingly rare on Galiano, as seedlings struggle to become established; for the most part only mature and old-growth trees remain, roots well established in swamplands; vulnerable living trees exhibit a white rot caused by the fungus *Obba rivulosa*; the name *Thuja* is derived from the Greek *thuia*, for an evergreen tree; in Hul'q'umi'num', the tree is called *xpey?*.

## Note:

All Indigenous nomenclature is taken from Appendix 2 of Nancy Turner's two-volume work *Ancient Pathways, Ancestral Knowledge: Ethnobotany and Ecological Wisdom of Indigenous Peoples of Northwestern North America* (Montreal: McGill-Queens University Press, 2014).

# Just. Don't. Say. It.

**TZEPORAH BERMAN**

After a long winter of rain in Vancouver, feeling battered by the storms and strange amount of snow and ice that our city is simply not set up to deal with, we have arrived on Cortes Island off the coast of British Columbia for a glorious month of walking the white-sand beaches and exploring one of the richest tidal lagoons on the West Coast. Manson Lagoon has been a special place for our family since our boys were little, when we moved back to British Columbia to find a place where Forrest and Quinn could grow up connected to nature. I will never forget explaining tides to Forrest, then four years old, when we first moved. That day, his preschool went to the lagoon to search for treasures. As the tide started trickling in I pointed it out to him, showed him the markings on the rocks ten feet up, and explained how the lagoon would fill and empty twice a day. Dropping his bucket in alarm, he took off for the beach faster than I have ever seen him run, yelling to his new friends: "The tide is coming! Run for your lives!" I doubled over trying not to laugh as I realized I hadn't explained how long it took for the tide to come in.

We look forward every summer to returning to Cortes. As the sun shines, we walk through the lagoon at low tide, amazed at the complexity of the ocean floor, gingerly stepping over clam beds, huge populations of sand dollars, and thousands of sharp oyster shells. This year, as we near one of our favourite spots, a small island that is usually crowded with life, it slowly dawns on us that we haven't seen a single starfish clinging to the rocks. Last year there were dozens, piled on top of each other in a glorious orange and purple display.

"Maybe it's just currents and they have moved," Quinn says, hopefully.

We continue to explore and eventually find two starfish, dying, cloudy, and soft. My stomach drops. I had read earlier in the year of increasing ocean acidification impacting the scallop industry, and I have seen projections of the impact of warming oceans on sea life for decades.

Staring down at the dying starfish, Forrest mumbles fiercely under his breath.

"Don't say it. Just. Don't. Say. It. Everything is not about climate change. Can you please just let us have this moment? This place?"

With an aching heart I realize, yet again, how hard it is for my boys to grow up at this moment in history, bombarded with the daily evidence of climate change. I want more than anything for my boys to be carefree, to feel like their future holds unlimited promise. Yet, every day, they are faced with news of unprecedented floods, fires, droughts. I can't stop thinking about how hard it is for this generation to manage the daily changes, the litany of disasters, the constant warnings. More than anything, I feel their cognitive dissonance: they live in a visibly warming world, but for the most part the adults around them continue on as though nothing has changed.

The following summer, we spend weeks inside because the blanket of smoke that has settled around our house is so thick we can't see the lake across the road or go outside without coughing. We read in horror about the hundreds of fires in BC and Alberta as we close our windows and cancel plans for hiking and kayaking. With anxious faces the boys ask us if everything will go back to normal, or if the smoke and fires are something we now have to plan around every year. They show me YouTube videos of people in Toronto having to swim off the King Street streetcar during flash flooding. We read articles together about people dying in Quebec due to heat waves. We watch, incredulous, as California burns.

"It's happening now, isn't it?" asks Forrest.

Quinn retreats into computer games, worlds that he can control.

They don't know who to support with their first federal election votes.

My activism is now infused with the anger of a mother bear. In this climate changing era, no one has all the answers. We need healthy debate and dialogue about how to build a new clean energy economy. Engineers, economists, and scientists tell us that we have the technology to make the changes we need and that inaction will cost us more. Yet here we sit in Canada, debating how to help the oil industry expand while our children watch the demise of the natural world on which we all depend.

Forrest and Quinn are watching their freedom go up in smoke. When I went to university, I had choices. I could be an artist, a musician, a scientist, a writer. Current climate projections tell us that we are on a trajectory to a world that could warm between four and six degrees: a level of warming that is already resulting in a massive increase in the severity and frequency of violent storms, that will lead to millions of people displaced. This year, the United Nations reported that more people lost their homes due to climate change than due to war. Around the world, many universities and schools were closed this year because of floods, droughts, heat waves.

Will our children have the luxury of studying a Mozart concerto, reading Plato, or losing themselves in the complexities of mycorrhizal fungi, when they are struggling for water? I want my children to be safe, but, perhaps even more, I want them to have the choices I had about who I could become and what I wanted to do.

———————

The mist is rising on Burnaby Mountain as the Indigenous Elders, singing and drumming, lead us toward the gates of the tank farm. As we arrive, I see many people I know: engineers, scientists, economists, and politicians take their place on the blockade. I go to speak to an elderly woman who is shaking with the cold as she limps to take her place.

"Are you sure you want to be doing this?" I ask her.

She looks up at Forrest, now six feet tall.

"I am a retired teacher. I am so sick of sitting at home and watching this happen. Right now, at this moment in history, there is no place I would rather be."

Forrest and I feel the same way. Taking action with those who feel the same way seems to alleviate some of our anxiety and despair. As I watch him this year, volunteering for the 350.org chapter at his university, organizing rallies on divestment, I am proud, but I am also sad that he feels he has to spend his free time this way when I know he would rather be skiing, climbing, or kayaking. I struggle with being honest with him when we talk about whether political change will happen quickly enough to reverse the warming trends we see all around us.

Quinn tells me that he is proud of my work on climate change. But he has retreated from the issues. He has stopped going to speeches and rallies, and, more often than not, he can be found debating game strategy with virtual teams of people in far-flung countries that he has met online. This activity is a relief for me, in some ways, but I also have to struggle to understand and accept it. We discuss over dinner whether virtual realities and communities are "real," and about how, for many people, the online world seems to be a relief from our ever-changing and threatening physical world.

In my activism, I have to face the science and politics of climate change every day. I run environmental campaigns to try to get decision-makers to change laws and policies to address the challenges we face. Progress is often slow. The changes in our energy system are now faster than they have ever been, and I think one of the keys to relieving anxiety in my boys is tracking and holding on to those signs of hope. On our good days, we have conversations about how exciting it is to be living in this moment of great change, and they talk about all the changes they are seeing around them: the cool electric cars and trucks, the high-speed rail, the big renewable energy projects. I tell them stories about how when I was in university there were no cellphones or internet and how quickly the world can change.

As I write this, hundreds of thousands of young people are marching, around the world, in student strikes for action on climate change. While I know we live in a warming world and will continue to see devastating changes in the places we love, I hope that we are truly living at the tipping point on climate change, driven by the engagement of youth.

# This Is the Way

## HIROMI GOTO

---

海

```
   y    k        p       o      o         p    t
ph t p an t on hy to  la kto  np yt plan ton  y op  n
   o  l     t   p   y   p   n    n   h     k     h    la
                      ファイト
```

川

nagare nagareru nagare nagare nagareta nagare nagaretai nagareru

雨

The way rain falls the spring of life seed to root, stem to leaves. Oh trees, weather maker, life shaper, air sweet. Language of snail, moss, lichen. Everything returns. Soil, water, particles in the air. To the deep sea vents. The strangest creatures, darkness, ocean breathes. Rising and falling, water, bull kelp, undulating forest. Sea. Everything seen and unseen. Holdfast, my kin, let all these relations.

水

Darkeyed you fly into morning
                                        light sweet song
          sparrow a tremble of notes liquid
                    larks red winged red finched
chickadee chickadee my heart
                              blooms this is the way sporophytes
            spores gemmae gemmae
oh my rhizoid stone transform
                              moss from water light this way
from seed to tree, sap to leaf, fur, crawl and creep


                                        splash!
      fish flash glisten the tail thrash against
the current water the current home salmon
                          this perfect berry, translucence
なんともいえない      sweet of sun sweet of water this is

the way the Salish Sea breathes the rising and falling
                      tide we breathe phytoplankton we
breathe gratitude a spray exhalation
                    bursts a baleen grin


    more herring than galaxies more eggs than stars this is the way

soft corals bull kelp mica quartz   かぞえないほど   かぞえないかず


            snails and clams, anemone, barnacles, eel grass see
gulls glide between water
                  sky alight my heart        the shore


                rain

hands mouth blood this is arbutus and oak, fiddlehead and fungi,
tule, cattails, the rushing air

ancient kinships and the gift of bees
flowering, roots and pollen
cedar,    sweet cedar, sweet grass, salal

this is the way we live

now

the 6th mass extinction event                    when permafrost

no longer

carbon sinks                    carbon rises
how a sinkhole explodes            tundra
beneath a rime of ice

a slurry of clay
oiling            the machine
a climate of our own                    making a climate

of fear            monstrous

unmaking the monster

change

# Q *da gaho dẹ:s*: Isle Weaving
# in Climates of Change

## TIMOTHY B. LEDUC

They preferred to walk in the darkness of war
[but] today the Sun dissipated all these clouds
to reveal that beautiful Tree of Peace
which was already planted on the highest mountain of the
   earth.

—Kondiaronk, Wendat Chief, 1701

---

*My thoughts move quickly, lock-stepped with the pace of concern about
unprecedented floods, forest fires, hurricanes, stalled political responses,
and communities of resistance. As I come into a patch of sunlight beyond
the tree cover, the flight of four eagles that chase and circle the Pacific
waterline stills everything.*

> *Thoughts stop and*
> *are silenced*
> *as two eagles perch*
> *in a Douglas-fir that reaches*
> *into the clear sky*

Standing below them, a fissure in time and space opens as I am
carried from this Pacific isle to another, thousands of kilometres
away, to another tree and time. In 1701, the respected Wendat Chief
Kondiaronk lifted a tall white pine as a "beautiful Tree of Peace"
for forty nations gathered on the isle of Montreal. His vision was
inspired by the five nations of the Haudenosaunee Confederacy who,

long before the colonial era, gathered under this tree to affirm peace following years of war, violence, and fear. Though the Wendat and Haudenosaunee had been fighting for at least a century, they were connected by the Peacemaker, who brought this Tree of Peace to the Haudenosaunee from his Wendat shores on the north side of Lake Ontario.

An eagle sat atop the white pine with a long-ranging sight to warn of approaching danger, and Kondiaronk hoped the sight of the forty nations was becoming as clear as the eagle's after so much colonial violence. Immersed in the calm climate of this tall evergreen and its winged guardians, Montreal's French host, Governor Louis-Hector de Callière, came forward with words to affirm the peace.

> I today ratify the peace we have made.
> I attach my words to the wampum belts
> I give to each of your nations
> so that the Elders may have them carried out by their
>     young people.

The negotiations were suffused with wampum belt teachings from the White Pine's Great Law, the Dish with One Spoon, and the Kaswenta, or Two Row, which dates to 1613 Mohawk-Dutch relations and its British adoption in 1677.

> Two rows of purple amidst white
> an Indigenous Canoe and European Ship
> going side-by-side
> down our Common Waters
> in a spirit of Peace,
> Friendship
> and Truth
> that is to last Forever.

*Not far from the Douglas-fir, a dark cable slithers up from the lapping wat-ers. It is kin to the energetic Black Snake that tries to hide below our oceans of desire for never-ending profit, economic growth and energetic mobility, even as it threatens the life-giving qualities of water, land, and climate.*

There is an interwoven nature to these injustices that the Ship sees as distinct. As the Truth and Reconciliation Commission high-lights, "the Canadian government pursued this policy of cultural genocide because it wished to divest itself of its legal and financial obligations to Aboriginal people and gain control over their *land and resources* [italics added]." This shadowy hull is what continues to inhibit a Canadian nation that tried to take global leadership at the 2016 Paris climate conference, but did so while touting pipeline developments like Keystone XL and Trans Mountain.

*Rough textured bark beneath my fingers shifts my awareness.*

I am called to that sacred space of *ǫ da gaho dẹ:s* that I often hear described by Cayuga Elder Norma Jacobs Gaehowako (Ancestral Women Holding the Canoe). As she teaches, between the Two Rows is a small vessel where Ship and Canoe are to meet and share under-standings that should inform a common way of Peace, Friendship, and Truth. In the words of the late Cayuga Chief Jacob Thomas:

> There is a bridge for all people to cross,
> a common belief to bring us together.
> There is only one Creator.

To approach this Bridge, Vessel, Isle, *Ǫ da gaho dẹ:s*, we need a humble spirit that can interweave our diverse cultural ways into relation through common responsibilities. If we are to stand together in the shade of this tree's green boughs and ensure it stays uplifted, our roots must be nourished by the life-sustaining waters.

The Montreal tree of Kondiaronk's vision would last only until French-British hostilities resurged a half-century later over control of the land's wealth, followed by the American Revolution and an emerging Canada that wilfully forgot such agreements. Perhaps Eagle saw the dark shadow around Callière's intent and subsequent colonial officials who held something untouchable in the Ship's hull. Did Eagle warn the Canoe of the violent pain that had already begun with religious missions across the river from Montreal in the Mohawk community of Kahnawá:ke? What about when those peace-shattering missions expanded with Canadian residential schools like the infamous Kuper Island Residential School? Or the 1960s "scooping of children" into foster homes by social workers who took over for the closing schools, a trend that continues today in the child welfare system? All of this rather than approach a sacred meeting on this isle, on *o da gaho dę:s*.

Though the institutions of the Ship change over time, its isolating hull continues to convert, create dependencies, emit disproportionate amounts of greenhouse gases, and manifest the chaos of so many climatic changes. These issues are not outside us, but are woven deep within: in our intensifying attachments to modern conveniences, ever-quickening pace, growing consumption of resources, rising intensity of travel as kilometres driven and flown increase each year, and packaged green consumerism.

Each of these tendencies reinforces my, our, disconnect from the painful uncertainties of forest fire infernos, flooding communities, pipeline threats to beautiful mountain ravines, a sunny West Coast day of protest. We are being taught about the vulnerabilities of the Ship's ways, of where real change begins.

*Don't leave the shores of this isle too soon. Slowing down to feel the ebbing ocean, cool wind blowing, and eagles resting in branches above, a question arises from these depths.*

*Can you sit against the Tree of Peace longer?*
*Can you learn of your responsibilities?*

Letting this call settle in, another image arises from the shadows as I notice Callière, a Frenchman, having wampum belts woven and gifted. It is an act that today seems the epitome of colonial appropriation, but what if his intent had been to learn the cultural protocols of our Common Waters? What if we engage him in this way, as one who wanted to approach ǫ da gaho dḜ:s? Can we walk such a renewed intent toward our climate of change?

*Not far from the Douglas-fir I can see in the forest understorey the snake-patterned leaves and greenish-white flowers of a rattlesnake plantain.*

The name of this indigenous orchid reminds me of Robin Wall Kimmerer's thoughts on the non-indigenous common plantain. Brought across the ocean on the Ship, its way of being is similar to that of other foreign plants, such as garlic mustard, which expands its range by poisoning the soil and growing without limits. While the Ship's ways also poison the water, land, and climate, this plantain has become part of Indigenous medicine bundles because it is useful in healing wounds and has found a place to fit in with the land's original inhabitants. It is not indigenous like the rattlesnake plantain but has become, as Kimmerer says, "naturalized" to Turtle Island relations. Here is some cultural medicine that can teach the Ship what it takes to be rewoven into the sharing spirit of ǫ da gaho dḜ:s.

*Great trees,*
*eagles above*
*plantains below*
*and a rising turbulence*
*in our Common Waters*

From these many beings, I am learning what is needed for us to come into ǫ *da gaho dę:s*; to affirm acts of being naturalized by our climate of change. In this sacred place and time, we are asked to embody values that can slow us down long enough to uncover the "truth" of colonial ancestries in our families and institutions—and find ways of reducing a consumptive drive that needs evermore fuel. The ways of the Ship must be pruned, made small and useful to life here. In the words of Kimmerer: "Being naturalized to place means to live as if this is the land that feeds you....Here you will give your gifts and meet your responsibilities."

*It is a plea that, if I listen closely, can be heard in the hoarse call of the two eagles as they take flight from the tree of peace and fly out of sight along the isle shores.*

## Notes:

Jacob E. Thomas and Terry Boyle, *Teachings from the Longhouse* (New York: Stoddart, 1997), 17, 131.

Haudenosaunee understandings of this chapter are also informed by Cayuga Elder Norma Jacobs, with whom I co-teach at Wilfrid Laurier University.

Truth and Reconciliation Commission of Canada, *Honouring the Truth, Reconciling for the Future: Summary of the Final Report of the Truth and Reconciliation Commission of Canada* (Winnipeg: Truth and Reconciliation Commission of Canada, 2015), 3.

Robin Wall Kimmerer, *Braiding Sweetgrass: Indigenous Wisdom, Scientific Knowledge and the Teachings of Plants* (Minneapolis: Milkweed Editions, 2013), 213–15.

# For the Deep Future

**STEPHEN COLLIS**

i

Pearl / shell of cloud
pale first thought
first bird burst whole
looking for the deep future
in old universe frozen creaturely
its ancient tusks now plastic
Halloween vampire teeth
only the scale is different
animals of lost fortunes pondering
what *their* future once looked like
from perch of *their* indentured past

Boundary walker
these things we've heard you whispering—
coal found in miners' mouths
canaries in and out of coal mines
tea stains / junk food / marxist
memorabilia / the small holes
the rain made in your magic coat
or *shell* in the common parlance
calcium carbonate excreted
extracellularly as a culture is
as middens mark inhabitation
of shores with remnant nacre
and prismatic residue showing

And the bent field of electricity?
Like Rilke blinking before
the Château de Muzot
before the train to Trieste
time and place intertwining:
there is nothing that does not see you
Orpheus photographed glancing back
flecks of light beaten from our bodies
if only we had shells, right?
So we could heft continents
on our backs back to Pangaea
the earth a boat with its own rhythm
and the beach just a shell we left behind

The ungraspable
sometimes grasps us
by the hand / or throat
the dark teeters the
warmth in my hand is
your hand
the sea is yet lightless
and completely arbitrary
the black breakers coming
one after another out of time
rhythmically combing the dark
with their tusks—white and very real
and lifting wave after wave to the shore


ii


I wall people up in this poem
to warn the future
not to come back—
they'd only find out whose fault it was
the silent river / the beat up lakes
the acid ocean's rise
dry heart of continents burnt
and my tomorrowing limbs to climb
mountains though it's hard
to care this month
to carve out a space for feeling
go west to islands
that at great time scales
peep in and out of the sea
sift glacier / forest / people

stand together on the strand
shell midden mole built
out from island
to nearby island to form
a land net for fish capture

Is it deep time we've been
dwelling upon—time lapse
migrations from Africa to
each edge's atoll? I want
to see instead the deep future
sing furthering / sing memory
of what we will or will not have done
via descendants long after we are gone
see the forest we won't be living in
see the cedars still standing in storm
see the things that do not need our intervention

# Keeping Watch at Kwekwecnewtxw

**RITA WONG & EMILY McGIFFIN**

Beyond the moneyed noise,
    arrests, the frenzied
    corporate media and the restless
       profit margins,

    stands Kwekwecnewtxw,
       the Coast Salish watch house,
    guarding land and water.

Here, these many hours,
    we are mountain protectors,
       rooting in with calm
    forbearance.

People come in waves,
       and sing of water.
         They bring food
    stoke fires,
       encourage, teach.

Our ancestors guide our offerings
    and flow through the songs
        for our great-granddaughters,

        *Humanity*
        *must stop*
        *fossil fuel*
        *expansion.*

Together we keep watch
    for the enemies
    whose national interest lies
    in frenzied exploitation, lies in
    Trans Mountain, Site C, Muskrat Falls, Keeyask,
    lies in hydro colonization, environmental racism

        lies in the iniquities of
        mega-dams and pipelines.

They risk bankrupting us
    with mass extinctions, cancers, sacrifice zones
        with the loss of our land's health,
    with the death of possibilities—
        kinship, coexistence,
        loving interactions.

What links mega-dams and pipelines?
    Greed. Short-sightedness. Relatives
    who don't understand or care.

Our prayer and ceremony, our watch
    protect the sacred places. They strengthen
    the community with our courage,
    with our deep love.

And so we keep the camps going, all of us,
moon after moon. It's part of something larger.

It's part of something humbling, uplifting.
We keep the camps going,
    the sacred fires going,
        the kitchens and the workshops,
          going on,

reciprocal,
        waxing, waning
            but determined.

We listen to each other, to the spirit
of the place, its magic and its commonplace,

    and at the closing of the day

Night teaches us
    peace,
    rest, and
    how to move
    slowly,
        finding
        that the moon offers light enough
        to make one's way
          down the paths
            to the creeks, the river.

The struggles here and elsewhere
    are connected by a truth:
        we must become better relatives
        with the earth. With each other.
        We cannot afford
        the alternative.

**Note:**

For more information on the Kwekwecnewtxw watch house, the myriad issues related to the Kinder Morgan Trans Mountain pipeline expansion project, and ongoing efforts to stop it, please see: https://protecttheinlet.ca/structure/ and https://www.facebook.com/mountainprotectors/.

# Tidal

**ZOE TODD**

---

It is humbling to move from Alberta to Central Canada, and now, to New Haven, Connecticut, on the northern coast of Long Island Sound. Where I grew up, thirty degrees Celsius was an anomaly in the summers. But as soon as I moved to Ottawa, in the summer of 2015, I was greeted by humidity and heat unfamiliar to me. While people from Southern and Eastern Ontario have long contended with their humid summers, my prairie body writhes in misery as the humidex climbs into the forties. This summer, when I moved down to the Eastern Seaboard, I was confronted anew with the fragility of my body and its inability to withstand heat. I am a winter person. I grew up building forts, sledding, running, playing, cycling, snow-shoeing and cross-country skiing in the snow. Minus forty degrees Celsius? No problem. Forty degrees Celsius? No thank you. But this heat is a reality I must contend with as the world shifts and global temperatures rise.

To help me understand this new climate (both local and temporal), I set out this autumn to spend as much time as possible by the water. I want to understand how the water, earth, and sky shape this coastal Atlantic city, in Quinnipiac lands. I want to understand these local relationships so that I can situate myself in the contingencies of now. I may never fully adapt to the heat of an eastern North American summer, but I can at least do my best to understand the relations that shape these places. So, I try to walk to the sea every other day or so. To learn from it. The prairies, after all, were once covered in a massive sea that stretched from the Gulf of Mexico to the Arctic Ocean. We are all, in our own way, oceanic and tidal.

I am learning the rhythms of the tide as it inches and sweeps its way through concrete barriers, eases past columns, and pours itself through wooden piles. At first, I am at a loss, here, where the coast is sectioned and partitioned in urban and industrial blocks, in turns broken up by fuel farms, yacht clubs, residential developments, sweeping colonial mansions, bridges, and other settler infrastructure. Access to the coast in Connecticut remains a fraught enterprise, one deeply shaped by the settler colonial history of this state through which white settlers explicitly refused African-American communities access to the state's beaches. Today, the majority of Connecticut's shoreline is private, and between industrial claims to the shore and private residential development, access to the water is a challenge for those unable to afford beachfront property.

In the 1950s, a turnpike was built on New Haven's waterfront, severing the city from the sea. Despite the crowded city shoreline, with its imposing turnpike and fuel tanks and decommissioned factories, a small stretch of nature preserve between the highway and the bay, in the heart of the harbour, allows you to ease yourself out into the sand dunes to greet the crabs and dragonflies as they bustle amidst the grasses and mud. I am used to vaster expanses of sand, stretching out along rocky islands and sliding into inlets and coves. But I am grateful, as a newcomer, to be able to access this precious stretch of sand and salt marsh, and to witness the entangled relations that enliven it in every season.

My first memory of a tide is hazy. My body is tiny and squat, and I am leaning over a tidal pool on a beach in Vancouver, marvelling at starfish and crabs and kelp. I imagine it is a universe unto itself, the water flashing with sunlight and ripples of wind. This is no prairie water pool: this is something entirely new and strangely familiar to my toddler heart. Flash forward a few years and I am on a beach with my sister on Galiano Island and we are scooping up sand dollars in our small hands, turning them over and over, marvelling at their magic. If only I knew what a rude way this was to greet a fellow astronaut. If only I could apologize for spinning those galaxies round and round over constellations of sand.

Back in the heart of New Haven, the tide is easily forgotten. The constant drone of cars on the highway cuts the city off from Long Island Sound physically and aurally. Downtown, you can smell nary the tang of kelp forest nor the hints of molluscs burrowing their way down into the sand only a mile away. But the tide keeps going, in and out, greeting the coast, hugging in close against the rocks and grasses. Egrets bob up and down, stretching out their wings. Little fish flash in the tidal ponds nestled in sandy depressions, and crabs scuttle sideways.

On the prairies, the tide is a distant cousin. The memory of its movements millions of years ago, when the sea stretched all the way from the Arctic to the Gulf of Mexico, still shapes some ancient part of being in those vast expanses, I am sure. In that ancient expanse of former sea, the memory of sea creatures is ruptured by intensive settler colonial extraction and development. But even in these days of profound ecological disorientation on the northern plains, the tide keeps pushing and pulling on the shores at the edges of our consciousness, moulding earth and life, reminding us to soften to the current. Even with all the efforts to forget the sea here in New Haven, to burden it with fuel farms and sewage plants, turnpikes, and overpasses, the sea continues to flood in and out of these insistent muddy pockets of salt marsh, grasses, algae, and oysters. And I am comforted by this refusal to let human constrictions stop a ceremony as old as the planet itself.

In late October, a heavy storm raises the tide higher than I've ever seen it in New Haven. The water rushes over the steel ramparts, floods the public pier. It spills over onto the street and creeps toward my neighbours' houses. Sea level is rising here at a rate of several millimetres per year, and the city has launched numerous studies and projects to address the impacts of sea level rise and climate change-induced storm surges on its coast. As the water inches toward my neighbours' homes, I think about what this little neighbourhood will look like in fifty years, or a hundred, two hundred, a thousand, a million years from now. Soon, like those ancient seas that once covered my home province, this expanse of land will be underwater, populated anew by algae, crustaceans, molluscs, and maybe even new creatures that develop in relation to this place over time. Watching the sea inch toward me, I am keenly aware of the contingency of this place. The movement of the tides underscores the flux that animates this place, a concept I come to through Leroy Little Bear's work on Blackfoot metaphysics:

> "The native paradigm consists of several key things," Little Bear begins. "One of them is constant motion or constant flux. The second part is everything consists of energy waves. In the native world, the energy waves are really the spirit. And it is the energy waves that know," he says, with a strong emphasis on the last word. "It is not you that knows. You know things because you are made up of energy waves or a combination thereof." (Little Bear, quoted in Hill, "Listening to Stones.")

I am not of this place, so I cannot even begin to speak for it. That is the work of communities that have co-constituted the coast of Connecticut far beyond settler time and constructs, including the Hammonassett, Lenape, Paugussett, Pequot, Quinnipiac, and Western Nehântick nations. My Indigenous nation, the Métis Nation, co-constitutes itself in lands far to the northwest of here. However, in embodying the ethic of flux that Little Bear outlines, I can try to embrace the contingency of the coast, water, tide, change, and to do my best to be in good relation as the coast reels from the impacts of colonial capitalist white supremacist environmental destruction. Even urban places deserve care, ceremony, reciprocity. What is abundantly clear is that our plural, entangled climate futures depend on extending reciprocity to relations in every terrain, atmosphere, and watershed.

So I sneak out after dark, with the wind whipping up trees around me, and I pad my way down to the pier. I want to see the full moon caress the water just this once. I want to know that, after all is said and done, there are still moon and sea and stars and sand. And that matters more than anything. Someday, maybe, some other order of beings will stare out at those tidal waves and wonder: Who else has gazed upward at this harvest moon?

Did they know they were lucky?

## Note:

Don Hill, "Listening to Stones," *Alberta Views*, September 1, 2008, https:// albertaviews.ca/listening-to-stones/.

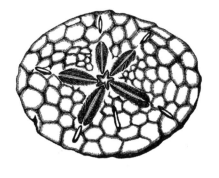

# Contributors

**CARLEIGH BAKER** is a nêhiyaw âpihtawikosisân / Icelandic writer who lives as a guest on the unceded territories of the xʷməθkʷəy̓əm, Skwxwú7mesh, and səlilwəta peoples. As an "urban" person of mixed ancestry, she has a complicated relationship to identity and to the land and often deals with both in her writing. Her debut short story collection, *Bad Endings*, won the City of Vancouver Book Award.

**SARA BARRON** completed her PHD in urban forestry at the University of British Columbia and has research experience in the areas of urban forests, urban planning and design, and landscape architecture. For a number of years, she worked on large-scale sustainable community planning and climate change research projects with both the Design Centre for Sustainability and the Collaborative for Advanced Landscape Planning at UBC.

**LOIS BEARDSLEE** (Anishinaabe = Lake Superior Ojibwe) grew up back and forth between rural northern Michigan and remote family bush camps in northern Ontario. She is the author of several books, including *The Women's Warrior Society*, and her traditional artwork is in public collections, including the Smithsonian Institution and the Royal Ontario Museum.

**TZEPORAH BERMAN**, BA, MES, LLD (*honoris causa*), has been designing and running environmental campaigns in Canada and around the world for over twenty-five years. She is a government adviser on climate policy, a writer, and a mom of two boys. She is the author, with Mark Leiren-Young, of *This Crazy Time: Living Our Environmental Challenge* (2011). She is also the international program director of Stand.earth. She lives in Vancouver, BC.

**CHRISTOPHER CAMPBELL-DURUFLÉ** is an attorney specializing in international environmental and human rights law, and a doctoral candidate at the University of Toronto. His research focuses on the different implementation mechanisms of the Paris Agreement and their potential to hold parties accountable. He has participated in the United Nations climate negotiations from COP 21 to COP 24, in the context of which he has supported and learned from the delegation of Burkina Faso.

**STEPHEN COLLIS**'s books of poetry include *The Commons* (Talonbooks, 2008, 2014), *On the Material* (Talonbooks, 2010), *Decomp* (with Jordan Scott, Coach House, 2013), and *Once in Blockadia* (Talonbooks, 2016). His most recent book, *Almost Islands* (Talonbooks, 2018), is a memoir of his friendship with poet Phyllis Webb. He lives near Vancouver, on unceded Coast Salish territory, and teaches poetry and poetics at Simon Fraser University.

**ALISON COLWELL** is a writer working primarily in the field of speculative fiction, a community organizer, and the manager of the Galiano Community Food Program, the mission of which is "building community through the medium of food." Alison Colwell lives on

Galiano with her family and a menagerie of animals, including a feral peacock. Find her at alisoncolwell.com.

**ASHLEE CUNSOLO** is a passionate researcher, environmental advocate, and community-engaged social science and health researcher working at the intersection of place, culture, health, and environment. She is a leader in the field of the mental and emotional impacts of climate change and ecological grief. She currently lives in Happy Valley-Goose Bay, on the homelands of the Innu and Inuit of Labrador, with her partner and their four boys.

**COLLEEN DOTY** is a writer and researcher living with her family on what is now known as Galiano Island. A three-time winner of the Surrey Young Adult Writing Contest, she writes poetry and short stories and is working on a novel. She has over twenty years' experience conducting research for modern and historical Indigenous claims. She is chair of the local seed library.

**ANN ERIKSSON**, author and biologist, has written five adult novels and two books for middle readers, *Dive In! Exploring Our Connection with the Ocean* (2018) and *Bird's Eye View: Keeping Wild Birds in Flight* (forthcoming in spring 2020). Her newest children's book project is about climate change migrants. Ann works for the Salish Sea Nearshore Habitat Recovery Project restoring eelgrass and shoreline ecosystems. She lives on Thetis Island, BC, and is a director of the Thetis Island Nature Conservancy. See https://www.anneriksson.ca/.

**SUZANNE FOURNIER** is a journalist and author who writes about Indigenous, environmental, and political history. Her 1998 book, *Stolen from Our Embrace*, was awarded the 1998 Hubert Evans Non-Fiction BC Book Prize. Her 2014 book, *Shore to Shore: The Art of Ts'uts'umutl Luke Marston*, is about Coast Salish and Portuguese-Canadian art and history. Suzanne has also written about Japanese-Canadian and Indigenous history on Galiano Island. She is a director of the Galiano Conservancy Association.

**ELYSIA FRENCH** is currently a post-doctoral fellow at York University in the Faculty of Environmental Studies. Her research examines the art and visual culture of climate change and its relations to public environmental understanding. This research builds on her doctoral work that examined visual narratives of the tar sands, as important modes of inquiry, in order to counter the tendency to render oil invisible.

**ROSEMARY A. GEORGESON** is a Sahtu Dene and Coast Salish writer, filmmaker, multimedia artist, and storyteller. Born and raised in a fishing family on what is now Galiano Island, her film *We Have Stories: Women in Fish* (2014) explored the role of women in the BC fishing industry. She was the 2014 Aboriginal Storyteller at the Vancouver Public Library. Most recently, she was co-author of the groundbreaking play *Weaving Reconciliation: Our Way* (2018).

**HIROMI GOTO** gratefully lives on the unceded territories of the Musqueam, Skwxwú7mesh, and Tsleil-Waututh Nations. She is the author of the novels *Chorus of Mushrooms* (1994), which won a Commonwealth Writers' Prize for best first book, and *The Kappa Child* (2001). She has also published poetry, short stories, and works for children and young adults, including *Half World* (2009). She's at work trying to decolonize her relationship to the Lands.

**LAURIE D. GRAHAM** grew up in Treaty 6 territory (Sherwood Park, Alberta), and she currently lives in Treaty 20 territory (Peterborough, Ontario), where she is a poet, an editor, and the publisher of *Brick* magazine. She has two books of poetry, *Rove* and *Settler Education*, and she recently published a collaborative chapbook with artist Amanda Rhodenizer called *The Larger Forgetting*.

**DEBLEKHA GUIN** is the founding executive director of Access to Media, an organization that uses digital media, creative collaboration, and facilitation to engage emerging change-makers in personally and socially transformative storytelling practices. A self-professed back-seat driver, she's much more at home supporting social and climate justice work from behind the scenes. She moved to Galiano Island after her second semester of graduate school in the early nineties and has lived there ever since.

**DYLAN M. HARRIS** is a PHD candidate in the Graduate School of Geography at Clark University. There, he studies the stories we tell (and don't tell) about climate change. Specifically, he is interested in how stories are used to construct climate knowledge and, more importantly, in the capacity for stories to transform our collective imagination about climate change. Find more information about him and his work at https://www.dylanmharris.com/.

**PETER HOBBS** is a doctor of philosophy, a master of fine art, and writer of fictions. He has published on a variety of subjects, including gay ghosts, dog pheromones, and a comic book ethnography, *The Tale of the Sarnia Nose* (2017). He has had solo exhibitions in Canada and the United States and has participated in group shows in Ireland, England, and Japan. Currently, Peter teaches drawing and thinking at OCAD University in Toronto.

**DAVID HUEBERT** is a self-styled dirty nature writer whose work has won the CBC Short Story Prize and the *Walrus* Poetry Prize, among other accolades. David's fiction debut, *Peninsula Sinking*, won the Jim Connors Dartmouth Book Award, was shortlisted for the Alistair

MacLeod Prize for Short Fiction, and was runner-up for the Danuta Gleed Literary Award. David recently completed a PHD on "species panic" in American literature. His second book of poetry, *Humanimus*, is forthcoming in 2020.

**SONNET L'ABBÉ** is a poet, professor, and songwriter. She is the author of *A Strange Relief, Killarnoe*, and *Sonnet's Shakespeare*. In 2014 she edited the Best Canadian Poetry anthology, and her work appears in many anthologies of Canadian verse. Her chapbook, *Anima Canadensis*, won the 2017 bpNichol Chapbook Award. She teaches creative writing and English at Vancouver Island University.

**TIMOTHY B. LEDUC** is author of the book *A Canadian Climate of Mind: Passages from Fur to Energy and Beyond* (McGill-Queen's University Press, 2016), which looks at the colonial roots of today's climate change–energy issues. He is faculty in land-based social work at Wilfrid Laurier University and has also published *Climate, Culture, Change: Inuit and Western Dialogues with a Warming North* (University of Ottawa Press, shortlisted for the 2012 Canada Prize in the Social Sciences).

**CHRISTINE LOWTHER** has authored three poetry collections and a memoir, *Born Out of This*, which was shortlisted for a BC Book Prize. She won the creative non-fiction category of the Federation of British Columbia Writers 2016 contest, Literary Writes, and the inaugural Rainy Coast Arts Award for Significant Accomplishment in 2014. Co-editor of two non-fiction anthologies, she happily contributes to other editors' projects now, especially those that work to save the planet.

**KYO MACLEAR** is an essayist, novelist, and children's author. Her books have been translated into sixteen languages and published in over twenty countries. She recently completed a PHD focused on climate change (York University) and is currently associate faculty with Humber College's School for Writers and the University of Guelph Creative Writing MFA program. Her most recent books are the hybrid memoir *Birds Art Life* and the graphic novel *Operatic*.

**LAUREN MAGNER** is an artist, care worker, and community organizer who is grateful to live as a guest on the traditional Coast Salish lands currently known as Galiano Island. The island's diverse and resilient forest, ocean, animal, and human communities inspire her work, art, and life. Her best friends are ferns, and her botanical art can be found at http://thelooseleafgaliano.ca/papery/.

**EMILY McGIFFIN** is the author of two books of poetry, *Between Dusk and Night* (Brick Books, 2012) and *Subduction Zone* (Pedlar Press, 2014); a third is forthcoming. Her scholarly book, *Of Land, Bones, and Money: Toward a South African Ecopoetics* (University of Virginia Press, 2019) examines the environmental politics of printed and oral isiXhosa poetry. She lives on Gitxsan territory in Hazelton, BC.

**DEBORAH McGREGOR** joined York University's Osgoode Hall law faculty in 2015 as a cross-appointee with the Faculty of Environmental Studies; she currently holds the Canada Research Chair in Indigenous Environmental Justice. Her research has focused on Indigenous knowledge systems and their various applications in diverse contexts, including water and environmental governance, environmental justice, health and environment, and climate justice. She is Anishinaabe from Whitefish River First Nation, Birch Island, Ontario.

**HILLARY McGREGOR** is the manager of Indigenous Sport and Wellness Ontario's Standing Bear youth leadership initiative. A graduate of Humber College's Sport Management program, he is currently a student in Georgian College's Anishnaabemowin and Program Development program, where he is learning more about his Anishinaabe language and culture. A resident of Toronto, Hillary maintains close ties with family members in Whitefish River First Nation, Birch Island, Ontario.

**EMILY MENZIES** has spent over twenty years co-creating workshops, trips, and classroom programs, and she helped establish the Millard Learning Centre on Galiano Island to equip the next generation of leaders to solve our climate crises. Now a mother and a secondary social studies teacher pursuing a master's degree in special education, Emily is researching how to mainstream a truly inclusive, ecology-based, restorative approach to our education system for Indigenous, settler, and newcomer young people.

**ASTRIDA NEIMANIS**, who grew up by the waters of Hamilton and Lake Ontario, is currently senior lecturer in gender and cultural studies at the University of Sydney on Gadigal land, in Australia. She writes mostly about water, weather, and bodies, often in collaboration with others. She is co-editor (with Cecilia Chen and Janine MacLeod) of *Thinking with Water* (2013) and author of *Bodies of Water: Posthuman Feminist Phenomenology* (2017).

**REBECCAH NELEMS** is a sixth-generation settler of Celtic descent on Stó:lō Nation land, currently living on Lekwungen territory with her two sons. She is a PHD candidate in sociology / cultural, social, and political thought at the University of Victoria, associate faculty with Royal Roads University's School of Leadership Studies, and a 2015 Pierre Elliott Trudeau scholar. Her dissertation asks: In this age of hyperconnectivity, with whom/what/where do people have a sense of kinship, connection, and belonging?

**REED OSLER** is a parks naturalist and environmental educator with over nineteen years' experience leading programs in parks, protected areas, and other wild spaces. She is currently the education coordinator at the Galiano Conservancy Association, where she facilitates day and multiday hands-on environmental education programs for both youth and adults. She includes a number of creative pursuits in her programs, including writing, song, and theatre.

**PHILIP KEVIN PAUL** is a W̱SÁNEĆ person who lives in W̱JOȽEȽP (Tsartlip). He has taught writing, English, and SENĆOŦEN and worked with the Canadian Institute of Ocean Sciences developing a comprehensive map of traditional W̱SÁNEĆ territory. His first book, *Taking the Names Down from the Hill*, won the BC Book Prize for poetry; his second, *Little Hunger*, was shortlisted for the Governor General's Award. He is currently completing a book based on traditional W̱SÁNEĆ stories.

**RICHARD PICKARD** lives and works as a settler on the traditional lands of the Lekwungen people. He teaches composition, literature, and the environmental humanities at the University of Victoria. Increasingly, and in solidarity with his students, his work has moved toward questions of climate change: in the classroom, in his research, and in his creative efforts.

**HOLLY SCHOFIELD** is a speculative fiction writer who travels through time at the rate of one second per second, oscillating between the alternate realities of city and country life. Her short stories have appeared in such publications as *Analog*, *Lightspeed*, and Canada's own *Tesseracts*, and have been translated into several languages. Recent climate fiction includes stories in *Cli-Fi: Canadian Tales of Climate Change* and *Glass and Gardens: Solarpunk Summers*. Find her at https://hollyschofield.wordpress.com.

**ANDREW SIMON** is an ecologist and naturalist dedicated to the Salish Sea bioregion, whose practice spans the socioecological continuum with a focus on the role of citizen science in biodiversity research. Currently, his research explores the implications of climate change for plant and pollinator communities of the Southern Gulf Islands. He continues to find room for more species in his heart as the curator of the Biodiversity Galiano project (http://biogaliano.org/) and beyond (https://salishseabiodiversity.org/).

**INDRA SINGH** is attempting to live convivially, learning from the many trees, flowers, ferns, fish, bushes, birds, snakes, spiders, and microfauna that she shares habitat with on beautiful Salt Spring Island, BC. She has published poetry in the *Capilano Review*. She is currently working on completing her PHD in environmental studies at York University, where she is on the Creative Review Team for *UnderCurrents* magazine.

**JAMIE SNOOK** was born in Mary's Harbour, Labrador, within the NunatuKavut territory of the Southern Labrador Inuit. As the long-standing executive director for the Torngat Wildlife, Plants and Fisheries Secretariat, he has a first-hand perspective on Indigenous co-management in Canada. Jamie is also a PHD candidate in public health at the University of Guelph's Department of Population Medicine.

**BERNARD SOUBRY** is a climate researcher, baker, and bike mechanic who lives and works between Montreal; Halifax, Nova Scotia; and Oxford, UK. A former farmer, he is completing a doctorate about how food systems adapt to climate change at the University of Oxford's Environmental Change Institute. His poems have previously been published in *Rise* and in other places. His technical writing about UN-level environmental negotiations occasionally appears in the *Earth Negotiations Bulletin*.

**LISA SZABO-JONES**, a photographer, writer, walker, scholar, and educator, grew up by the Salish Sea. She co-founded *The Goose: A*

*Journal of Arts, Environment, and Culture in Canada.* She is a co-editor of the collections *Activating the Heart* and *Sustaining the West* and of an ARIEL special issue, *Postcolonial Ecocriticism among Settler-Colonial Nations.* She is published in *Canadian Literature,* ISLE, *Alternatives Journal,* ESC, and *Greening the Maple.*

**JESSE THISTLE** is Métis-Cree from Saskatchewan, raised in Toronto. He is a PHD candidate in history at York University. His work on Métis road allowance communities won 2016 Pierre Elliott Trudeau and Vanier scholarships. He is also a Governor General's medalist. Jesse is the author of the "Definition of Indigenous Homelessness in Canada," published through the Canadian Observatory on Homelessness, and his memoir *From the Ashes* was published by Simon and Schuster in 2019. His Twitter handle is @Michifman.

**ZOE TODD** is a Métis artist and scholar from amiskwaciwâskahikan (Edmonton), Canada. She writes about fish, science, art, prairie fossilscapes, Métis legal traditions, the Anthropocene extinction, and decolonization in urban and prairie contexts. Her current work focuses on the relationships between people, fish, and other non-human kin in the context of colonialism, environmental change, and resource extraction in Treaty 6 Territory, Alberta, and the Lake Winnipeg watershed more broadly.

**BETSY WARLAND** has published twelve books of creative non-fiction, lyric prose, and poetry. Her 2010 book *Breathing the Page* became a bestseller. Her most recent book is *Oscar of Between: A Memoir of Identity and Ideas* (2016). Nature is present in all her books, and she is currently writing about Lost Lagoon in Stanley Park, Vancouver. Director of Vancouver Manuscript Intensive, she received the City of Vancouver Mayor's Arts Award for Literary Arts in 2016.

**EVELYN C. WHITE** is the author of *Every Goodbye Ain't Gone: A Photo Narrative of Black Heritage on Salt Spring Island* (2009) and of the biography *Alice Walker: A Life* (2004). She is an alumna of the Columbia University Graduate School of Journalism, where she was honoured for her master's thesis on "The Racial Development of Blind Black Children." She also holds degrees from Harvard University and Wellesley College.

**LEVI WILSON** is a teacher in the Greater Victoria School District, who completed his bachelor of arts in First Nations studies and history and bachelor of education in Indigenous perspectives at Simon Fraser University in 2016 and 2017, respectively. He is a member of the Gitga'at (Hartley Bay) First Nation, with strong familial ties to the Hwlitsum (Lamalcha) First Nation. Until recently, he had the privilege of living within his southern traditional territory, including his home community on Galiano Island.

**RITA WONG** co-edited *Downstream: Reimagining Water* (with Dorothy Christian). She has written six books: *Beholden* (with Fred Wah), *Perpetual* (with Cindy Mochizuki), *Undercurrent*, *Sybil Unrest* (with Larissa Lai), *Forage*, and *Monkeypuzzle*. Arrested for her principled opposition to the Trans Mountain pipeline expansion, Wong is also active in solidarity efforts to protect the Peace Valley from being destroyed by the Site C dam as well as calling for BC and Canada to respect Wet'suwet'en law and land.

# Other Acknowledgements

## CATRIONA SANDILANDS

The words that open *Rising Tides*—Levi Wilson's acknowledgement of the lands that are now known as Galiano Island, BC—were the first words spoken at a workshop held on the island in March 2018, in which many of the contributors to this volume participated.

Following Levi's guidance both there and here, I acknowledge that this volume is entirely enabled by the privilege of living, learning, and caring for one another, the land, and the water in the traditional and ongoing territories of the Penelakut, Lamalcha, and Tsawwassen peoples. As a volume that includes many other places, *Rising Tides* is also enabled by many other such privileges: as a settler who lives both on Galiano and in the area known as Tkaronto, then, I also acknowledge my reliance on the ongoing care-work of the Anishinabek Nation, the Haudenosaunee Confederacy, the Huron-Wendat, and the Métis. I am obliged to many treaties in these places, and one of my great hopes for this volume is that it might help us remember what it means to live up to them, especially in these climate changing times. For settlers like me, as Emily Menzies points out, this means living "as if we mean to stay," as well as remembering that these lands and waters remain unceded and that we are, at best, guests: may we settlers start to be much better guests.

*Rising Tides*, and the workshop that helped give it shape, are part of a Fellowship project, Storying Climate Change, supported by the Pierre Elliott Trudeau Foundation (PETF). I am grateful to the PETF for its funding and for its support of the many PETF scholars and former scholars who have made such important contributions to both the project and the book. I am also very grateful to the Faculty of Environmental Studies at York University for its support, as well as to my colleagues and students for their understanding of my absences (and their tolerance of all of the Zoom and Skype meetings) so that I could engage in the slow work of community-based collaboration.

Even as it includes contributions from many places, this volume obviously has a beating heart on Galiano Island. My overwhelming thanks to this extraordinary community: to the Galiano Conservancy Association, the Galiano Club and Community Food Program, the Galiano Writers' Group, the Galiano Library, and the many other individuals, organizations, and businesses who gave material, intellectual, and emotional support to the workshop (including exceptional food and inspiring music), to the volume, and to me over the three years it took me to complete the project.

I am in debt to Emily McGiffin and Betsy Warland, who supported the workshop from lofty design ideas to nuts-and-bolts delivery, and who also made invaluable contributions to the book through their extensive editorial support. Thank you to Elysia French for her design of the Storying Climate Change website and her work to provide a visual counterpoint to our words throughout the project, and to Deblekha Guin for her exquisite drawings throughout *Rising Tides*. And, of course, my thanks to all of the workshop and book contributors for their efforts on this volume and beyond: it is my privilege to know and work with such a truly brilliant group of passionate, thoughtful, creative people. Finally, my gratitude to Caitlin Press for its enthusiastic support of *Rising Tides*, and for its excellent stewarding of the collection to publication: Vici Johnstone, Holly Vestad, Sarah Corsie, thank you!